VMware Horizon View High Availability

Design, develop, and deploy a highly available
vSphere environment for VMware Horizon View

Andrew Alloway

PUBLISHING

BIRMINGHAM - MUMBAI

VMware Horizon View High Availability

Copyright © 2015 Packt Publishing

First published: November 2015

Production reference: 1121115

Published by Packt Publishing Ltd.
Livery Place
35 Livery Street
Birmingham B3 2PB, UK.

ISBN 978-1-78528-739-8

www.packtpub.com

Cover Image by Barry Alloway and Stuart Alloway

Credits

Author
Andrew Alloway

Reviewers
Bruce Bookman
Matthew Bunce
John Hubert

Commissioning Editor
Neil Alexander

Acquisition Editors
Shaon Basu
Manish Nainani

Content Development Editor
Arshiya Ayaz Umer

Technical Editor
Pramod Kumavat

Copy Editors
Ting Baker
Roshni Banerjee

Project Coordinator
Shipra Chawhan

Proofreader
Safis Editing

Indexer
Priya Sane

Production Coordinator
Nitesh Thakur

Cover Work
Nitesh Thakur

About the Author

Andrew Alloway was born and raised in Edmonton, Canada. He graduated from the University of Alberta with a computer science degree.

While working at Nuna Logistics Limited, he supported northern mining sites for their unique and challenging IT environment. In 2012, some of his projects and work were featured in the Winter 2012 edition of Aptitude Magazine in an article entitled "Building the road to streamlined license agreements".

He is a supporter of open source technology and products such as Ubuntu, ICTFax, Apache, Drupal, and Piler, among other projects.

He has designed and implemented projects, which include Exchange migrations, Lync deployments, System Center Configuration Manager, and various VMware products.

In 2013, he received the VMware Certified Professional 5 Data Center Virtualization certification.

He has previously worked with Packt Publishing on *VMware Horizon Workspace Essentials* and *VMware Horizon View High Availability*.

I would like to thank my family for all the support that I have received over the years and my employers for investing in the development of my skills and career.

About the Reviewers

Bruce Bookman is a Silicon Valley software and hardware veteran who has held roles from front-line technical support to the director of a software quality assurance. Recently, he has been VMware subject matter expert and a Level 3 technical support escalation engineer for a solid state storage company named Fusion-io. In late August 2014, he joined Oracle as a senior quality analyst for Oracle Cloud. He is the author of technical articles that cover virtualization and which are available on http://www.developer.com/. He created and delivered in-depth technical training on virtualization and several other topics. He has received a number of recognitions for customer advocacy and dedication towards customers' success.

John Hubert has been working in the IT industry since 2009 and has experience working in both MSP and corporate IT environments. John's expertise ranges from systems and network administration on a wide range of technologies to team management, client service, and technical writing.

John studied at DePaul University in Chicago, majoring in information systems. He got his feet wet in the industry at an MSP based in Chicago, where he was an IT manager. His focus was on datacenter implementations and the deployment of new technologies. His current focus is on networking. He co-manages the network of an enterprise-level technical consulting e-discovery firm headquartered in Washington DC.

John currently lives in Chicago. He enjoys the Chicago Cubs when they're winning, video games, and going outdoors as much as the chaotic Chicago weather allows. *VMware Horizon View High Availability* is John's first technical book review.

I'd like to thank UJ, Debbie, Robyn, and Lauren for always being there and of course, last but not least, mom.

www.PacktPub.com

Support files, eBooks, discount offers, and more

For support files and downloads related to your book, please visit www.PacktPub.com.

Did you know that Packt offers eBook versions of every book published, with PDF and ePub files available? You can upgrade to the eBook version at www.PacktPub.com and as a print book customer, you are entitled to a discount on the eBook copy. Get in touch with us at service@packtpub.com for more details.

At www.PacktPub.com, you can also read a collection of free technical articles, sign up for a range of free newsletters and receive exclusive discounts and offers on Packt books and eBooks.

https://www2.packtpub.com/books/subscription/packtlib

Do you need instant solutions to your IT questions? PacktLib is Packt's online digital book library. Here, you can search, access, and read Packt's entire library of books.

Why subscribe?

- Fully searchable across every book published by Packt
- Copy and paste, print, and bookmark content
- On demand and accessible via a web browser

Free access for Packt account holders

If you have an account with Packt at www.PacktPub.com, you can use this to access PacktLib today and view 9 entirely free books. Simply use your login credentials for immediate access.

Instant updates on new Packt books

Get notified! Find out when new books are published by following @PacktEnterprise on Twitter or the *Packt Enterprise* Facebook page.

Table of Contents

Preface

The increasing movement towards virtualized workloads and workstations has put VMware Horizon View into a central, mission-critical role in many environments. Administrators may be overwhelmed with planning for outages and dealing with failure-related scenarios. It's easy to miss small details that may result in outages down the road. Following VMware Horizon View best practices and planning ahead with network infrastructure will allow you to avoid these common pitfalls.

This book will walk you through the setup and configuration of View in a highly available configuration. It will provide you with the skills needed to analyze and deploy configurations that can stand up to rigorous failure standards.

What this book covers

Chapter 1, VMware Horizon View 6.0 Connection Server HA, covers the installation and configuration of a redundant pair of View connection servers.

Chapter 2, VMware View 6.0 Security Server HA, covers the installation and configuration of a pair of View security servers. We will also go through the firewall and DMZ requirements.

Chapter 3, Load Balancers and Deployment Planning, reviews the advantages and disadvantages of the various load-balancing technologies available for VMware Horizon View. Port configuration for load balancers is also covered.

Chapter 4, HA Planning for Floating and Dedicated Pools, covers stateless and stateful desktop deployments and the various pool types. HA is considered for each scenario, and useful tips and best practices are provided in this chapter.

Chapter 5, Storage HA with VMware Virtual SAN, provides an overview of VMware Virtual SAN and how it can be used to provide high availability for a Horizon View environment.

Chapter 6, Hardware Redundancy Planning for Fibre Channel Storage, covers the various topics related to Fibre Channel High Availability and the hardware requirements for deployments.

Chapter 7, NFS, iSCSI, and Network Planning, covers network-related High Availability concerns, which include DNS, Active Directory, DHCP, NFS, and iSCSI. Redundant switch configurations are covered along with VMkernel configuration concerns.

Chapter 8, Monitoring VMware Horizon View, covers the health monitoring of the View connection servers, vSphere hosts, and vCenter host. This chapter covers the usage of vRealize for Horizon View to perform an in-depth monitoring.

Chapter 9, Upgrade and Downtime Planning, covers a basic overview of upgrade planning and its common pitfalls. This chapter will help you minimize your downtime during maintenance windows.

What you need for this book

You will need the following:

- The licensed copies of VMware Horizon View
- A licensed copy of vSphere and vCenter
- 5 Windows Server licenses
- A minimum space of 500 GB and a RAM of 32 GB on a server platform
- For Virtual SAN, you need 3 ESXi hosts and Virtual SAN licenses
- Appropriate networking equipment and a minimum of Gigabit networking

Who this book is for

It is assumed that you have basic knowledge of VMware Horizon View and VMware vSphere ESXi. We will cover topics related to deployment planning and focus on High Availability and uptime concerns. It is recommended that readers purchase a copy of *VMware Horizon View 6 Desktop Virtualization Cookbook*, Packt Publishing, for an in-depth look at all the features of VMware Horizon View. All the steps in this book are intended for testing and development environments to build the skills related to High Availability. It is recommended that you read the entire book before planning and deploying a production VMware Horizon View environment.

Conventions

In this book, you will find a number of text styles that distinguish between different kinds of information. Here are some examples of these styles and an explanation of their meaning.

Code words in text, database table names, folder names, filenames, file extensions, pathnames, dummy URLs, user input, and Twitter handles are shown as follows: "Check whether the DNS round robin is working via `nslookup`."

Code and value fields noted for editing are displayed in the following format:

```
NFS.HeartbeatFrequency = 12
NFS.HeartbeatTimeout = 5
NFS.HeartbeatMaxFailures = 10
```

New terms and **important words** are shown in bold. Words that you see on the screen, for example, in menus or dialog boxes, appear in the text like this: "On the **Welcome to the Installation Wizard for VMware Horizon View Composer** window, hit **Next**."

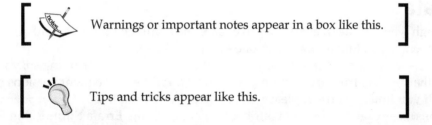

> Warnings or important notes appear in a box like this.

> Tips and tricks appear like this.

At the end of each chapter will be a checklist of items to go over to ensure the environment meets best practices. Ensure that any outage or failover testing is conducted in a test environment or pre-production environment.

- Power off each DNS Server, one at a time
- Power off each DHCP Server, one at a time, and verify that DHCP addresses are still being allocated
- Power off each domain controller, one at a time

Reader feedback

Feedback from our readers is always welcome. Let us know what you think about this book—what you liked or disliked. Reader feedback is important for us as it helps us develop titles that you will really get the most out of.

To send us general feedback, simply e-mail feedback@packtpub.com, and mention the book's title in the subject of your message.

If there is a topic that you have expertise in and you are interested in either writing or contributing to a book, see our author guide at www.packtpub.com/authors.

Customer support

Now that you are the proud owner of a Packt book, we have a number of things to help you to get the most from your purchase.

Downloading the example code

You can download the example code files from your account at http://www.packtpub.com for all the Packt Publishing books you have purchased. If you purchased this book elsewhere, you can visit http://www.packtpub.com/support and register to have the files e-mailed directly to you.

Errata

Although we have taken every care to ensure the accuracy of our content, mistakes do happen. If you find a mistake in one of our books—maybe a mistake in the text or the code—we would be grateful if you could report this to us. By doing so, you can save other readers from frustration and help us improve subsequent versions of this book. If you find any errata, please report them by visiting http://www.packtpub.com/submit-errata, selecting your book, clicking on the **Errata Submission Form** link, and entering the details of your errata. Once your errata are verified, your submission will be accepted and the errata will be uploaded to our website or added to any list of existing errata under the Errata section of that title.

To view the previously submitted errata, go to https://www.packtpub.com/books/content/support and enter the name of the book in the search field. The required information will appear under the **Errata** section.

Piracy

Piracy of copyrighted material on the Internet is an ongoing problem across all media. At Packt, we take the protection of our copyright and licenses very seriously. If you come across any illegal copies of our works in any form on the Internet, please provide us with the location address or website name immediately so that we can pursue a remedy.

Please contact us at copyright@packtpub.com with a link to the suspected pirated material.

We appreciate your help in protecting our authors and our ability to bring you valuable content.

Questions

If you have a problem with any aspect of this book, you can contact us at questions@packtpub.com, and we will do our best to address the problem.

1

VMware Horizon View 6.0 Connection Server HA

In this chapter, we will examine and deploy VMware Horizon View Connection servers configured in a High Availability pair. We will cover the function of the vCenter server, View Composer, and View Connection server. We will examine topologies that can be used to provide High Availability to the View components and tips on how to deploy them. We will cover DRS rules and power on procedures. We will also cover basic service requirements to provide highly available network resources required by View.

In this chapter, we will discuss the following topics:

- Licensing Horizon View
- Database considerations for Horizon View
- Functions of the vCenter server for View
- Functions of the View Composer
- Installation of the View Composer
- Functions of the View Connection servers
- Installation of View Connection servers
- Network Services HA
- Failure testing

Licensing Horizon View

There are multiple license models for VMware Horizon View. Here, we used Horizon View Standard Edition for most of the functionality, but you will require Horizon View Advanced Edition to utilize VMware Virtual SAN technology.

 You can review the license features at: `http://www.vmware.com/products/horizon-view/compare.html`

VMware vSphere is required for use in this book. VMware Horizon View can be used with all editions of vSphere but I would strongly recommend vSphere Enterprise, vSphere Remote Office Branch Office Standard, or vSphere Essentials Plus Kit levels of licensing for access to **Distributed Resource Schedule (DRS)** and DRS Rules. DRS is essential to ensure that hosts are properly balanced within a cluster and that VMs are bound to the correct host. High Availability is also required to bring VMs up after a host failure.

 You can review the vSphere editions on VMware's website at `http://www.vmware.com/products/vsphere/compare.html`.

For VMware Horizon View, you will need to license Windows Enterprise Edition for the Client Desktops and have a Microsoft KMS (short for Key Management Service) activation server deployed.

 Microsoft has released a guide on configuring KMS licensing hosts available here:

`https://technet.microsoft.com/en-us/library/ff793409.aspx`

For Windows servers, you will need at least three licensed copies; up to five are used in this book. You will need the following components on separate Windows servers: vCenter, View Composers, View Security server, Active Directory servers, and any redundant pairs. Each server should be licensed with a Windows Server Standard license.

For Microsoft databases, you will need either a Microsoft SQL Standard or higher license for High Availability or use the Express Edition.

For licensing information about Oracle databases, please review the Oracle documentation regarding licensing at http://www.oracle.com/us/corporate/pricing/sig-070616.pdf.

Database considerations for Horizon View

Every highly available application requires a highly available database, and VMware Horizon View is no exception.

The View Composer supports both Microsoft SQL Server and Oracle.

 Note that not all versions of vCenter support the same database versions that the View Composer does.

The following table lists the databases compatible with the View Composer and various versions of vCenter:

Database	Database High Availability	vCenter Server 6.0	vCenter Server 5.5	vCenter Server 5.1	vCenter Server 5.0	vCenter Server 4.1
Microsoft SQL Server 2014 Standard and Enterprise (32- and 64-bit)	Yes	Yes	Yes	No	No	No
Microsoft SQL Server 2012 Express (32- and 64-bit)	No	Yes	Yes	Yes	Yes	No
Microsoft SQL Server 2012 (SP1) Standard and Enterprise (32- and 64-bit)	Yes	Yes	Yes	Yes	Yes	No
Microsoft SQL Server 2008 Express (R2 SP2) (64-bit)	No	Yes	Yes	Yes	Yes	No
Microsoft SQL Server 2008 (SP3), Standard, Enterprise, and Datacenter (32- and 64-bit)	Yes	No	No	Yes	Yes	Yes
Microsoft SQL Server 2008 (R2 SP2), Standard and Enterprise (32- and 64-bit)	Yes	Yes	Yes	Yes	Yes	Yes
Oracle 10g Release 2, Standard, Standard ONE, and Enterprise [10.2.0.4] (32- and 64-bit)	Yes	No	No	Yes	Yes	Yes

Database	Database High Availability	vCenter Server 6.0	vCenter Server 5.5	vCenter Server 5.1	vCenter Server 5.0	vCenter Server 4.1
Oracle 11g Release 2, Standard, Standard ONE, and Enterprise [11.2.0.3] (32- and 64-bit)	Yes	Yes	Yes	Yes	Yes	Yes
Oracle 12C, Standard, ONE Edition, Enterprise, Release 1 [12.1.0.1.0] - 64-bit	Yes	Yes	Yes	No	No	No

 Check out the VMware Product Interoperability Matrixes for more details:

`http://www.vmware.com/resources/compatibility/sim/`
`interop_matrix.php`

With the flexibility of VMware vSphere comes multiple ways to approach High Availability for databases. We can utilize VMware High Availability to ensure that database VMs are protected in the event of host failure. We can utilize database clusters to ensure that the database is always available and to provide load balancing. We can also use active-passive configurations to provide access to the database in the event of a failure.

As with all systems, good backups of the databases are essential to get things running again in the event of a disaster.

Functions of the vCenter server

VMware vCenter Server is the heart of most VMware products. It manages the VMs and hosts of the datacenter. For VMware Horizon View, vCenter is essential to allocating new VMs and balancing the VMs across multiple hosts. vCenter also manages the power state of View VMs and the resource allocation.

vCenter is required for the following functions to work:

- **Power on/off/reset**: vCenter will power on, off, or reset all the VMs in the View environment.
- **VMware High Availability**: vCenter is responsible for configuring hosts to act in an appropriate manner in the event of a host failure. In the event of a host failure, the failure will be detected and VMs will be restarted on working hosts.

- **VMware vMotion**: vCenter is responsible for migrating VMs between hosts in a cluster.

- **VMware DRS**: vCenter will monitor host resources and can automatically migrate VMs between hosts to balance the load. DRS can also be used to separate redundant VMs to ensure that the system continues to operate in the event of a host failure. DRS should be implemented on clusters where shared storage is used, such as Virtual SAN or any SAN or NAS configuration. DRS is not required for clusters where the hosts only have local storage.

- **View Composer**: vCenter is required by the View Composer to accomplish any task managing the link-cloned desktops.

High Availability deployment scenarios for vCenter

There are several options for deployments of vCenter, depending on the size of the environment size. I will illustrate several deployment situations here and discuss how we can provide High Availability for vCenter.

Small deployments

We will examine the use case of small offices and remote office deployments for VMware View. Typically, this revolves around small companies who do not possess large datacenters. We are looking at deploying servers on a small budget and are looking for ways to cut costs as much as possible. This is also applicable for small satellite offices or locations where VMware Horizon View over the Internet is not feasible.

This environment will have less than 50 VMs, 2 ESXi hosts, local storage only, along with vSphere replication.

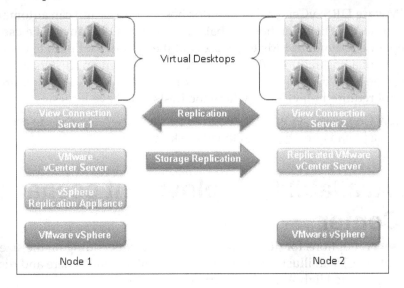

This is a typical environment for small VMware View deployments with the minimal size. Here, we will utilize vCenter licensed with vSphere Remote Office Branch Office Standard or vSphere Essentials Plus. ESXi hosts have locally attached hard drives or SSDs or both. We have several options for deploying vCenter. We can install vCenter on a single VM with a collocated database and View Composer. To protect this VM, we utilize VMware Replication Appliance to copy the vCenter to the other host frequently. In this situation, we simply power on the vCenter replica on the other host in the event of a host failure. Note that data loss from the vCenter may occur since the replication may be out of sync. This can be acceptable for some View scenarios, since vCenter configurations rarely change. Note that a failure and recovery from the replicated vCenter may require VMware technical support to recover. This is due to the databases potentially being out of sync with ESXi hosts and other VMware products.

We can also utilize an alternative configuration using SQL Replication instead of relying on vSphere Replication. This configuration requires two licenses of the chosen database (Microsoft Standard or Enterprise Edition or Oracle database). This scenario is suitable for small offices, satellite offices, and offices where Horizon View over the Internet isn't an option. This configuration has a higher reliability than the scenario above at the cost of an extra database license.

This environment will have less than 50 VMs with 2 ESXi hosts, local storage only, and SQL replication.

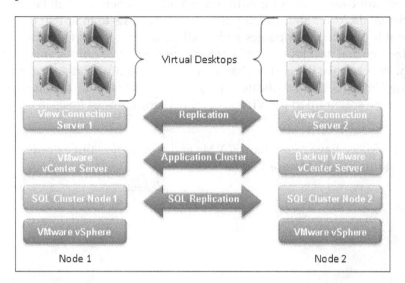

Here, we install the vCenter database and the View Composer database on the chosen database cluster.

The vCenter server will host our View Composer. We can either replicate the vCenter VM using the vSphere Replication Appliance, take frequent backups using VMware Data Protection, or use a third-party backup solution. This solution benefits from not losing any database data. In the event of a host failure, recovery can be configured to be automated in with Application Clustering solutions.

With vCenter Server 5.5 Update 3 and later, Windows Server Failover Cluster is supported as an option for providing vCenter Server availability. Two instances of vCenter Server are in a MSCS cluster, but only one instance is active at a time. VMware only supports two node clusters.

We can also utilize a third-party application clustering to manage the services on two vSphere hosts such as Symantec ApplicationHA using an Active Backup configuration.

Medium-to-large deployments

Here, we examine use cases for medium-sized offices where we will be running more than 50 virtual desktops and utilizing three or more hosts to maintain the load. This deployment is typical of companies with dedicated datacenters who want to deploy a centralized virtual desktop scenario, remote medium-size offices, small schools, and so on. We can save the cost of shared storage and simplify the recovery scenario by utilizing Virtual SAN to replicate copies of all the VMs onto separate hosts. This scenario can be scaled up to the Virtual SAN maximums of 64 hosts in 6.0 and 32 hosts in 5.5.

In this scenario, we have more than 50 VMs and will deploy three or more ESXi hosts with local storage and VMware Virtual SAN.

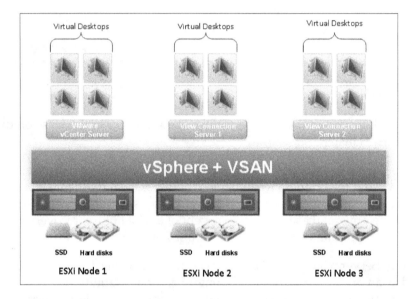

In a 3+ node cluster, we open up the option to use VMware Virtual SAN to protect the data stores of the ESXi hosts. By placing vCenter on the Virtual SAN datastore, we can utilize VMware High Availability to protect the vCenter server in the event of a host failure. While a second View Connection server is somewhat redundant in this scenario, I recommend two so that one will always be running in the event of a host failure. Virtual desktops can be stored on the Virtual SAN or on local storage depending on the High Availability and data requirements for the virtual desktops.

Shared storage deployments

In case of shared storage deployments, we opt for a shared storage solution for our ESXi cluster. Shared storage can be required for applications that are not designed with High Availability in mind to provide redundancy or to simplify the failover scenario where high percentage uptime is not a large concern. This could be Fibre Channel SAN, NFS, and iSCSI. With three or more hosts, we can utilize Virtual SAN as our shares storage as outlined in the previous scenario.

Shared storage simplifies the High Availability plan, since it is often as easy as turning on VMware High Availability to protect the cluster and ensuring there is enough capacity to work in a failover scenario. When using shared storage, make sure to configure DRS on the cluster to ensure that redundant VMs are kept on separate hosts.

Here, we have two or more ESXi hosts with shared storage:

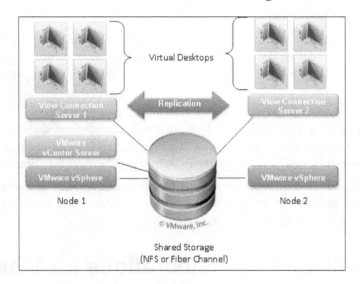

The shared storage scenario shares much of the same topology as the Virtual SAN scenario. By placing vCenter on the shared data stores, we can utilize VMware High Availability to protect the vCenter server in the event of a host failure. While a second View Connection server is somewhat redundant in this scenario, I recommend two so that one will always be running in the event of a host failure. Virtual desktops can be stored on shared or local storage, depending on the High Availability and data requirements for the virtual desktops.

Functions of the View Composer

The View Composer is used to manage virtual desktops on the vCenter server. Its primary function is to track link-cloned desktops and manage the state and configuration of link-cloned desktops. Link-cloned desktops share the same OS disk, providing a significant storage saving over fully-provisioned persistent virtual desktops. Link-cloned desktops consist of a VMDK that is used to track changes to the OS disk, and a user data VMDK when configured for persistent user disks.

Fully provisioned desktops can be deployed manually by installing a Client OS on a VM or using the View Composer to provision virtual desktops that are cloned from a base. Fully provisioned desktops use the same amount of disk space as the base image if thick provisioned or if thin provisioned the OS disk usage plus the user's data.

The View Composer handles the following requests from the View Administration Console:

- **Refresh**: This action restores linked clones back to their original size and state. This reduces the size of clones that can grow over time and simplifying the removal of undesirable changes to the operating system, while preserving user profiles.

- **Recompose**: This action pushes a new version of an image to all users in the assigned pool. It is useful for deploying complicated software and patches that many users in a pool require. This operation also removes undesirable changes from the operating system, while preserving user profiles.

- **Rebalance**: This action allows the systems administrator to manage the location of View Link-Cloned desktops. A rebalance is required to migrate View VMs to other datastores/hosts.

High Availability considerations for View Composer

A View Connection server only needs access to the View Composer for recomposing images and refreshing VMs. View only needs access to vCenter to power on/off VMs and to complete any operation that the View Composer is required for.

For small environments, it is often acceptable to have outages on the View Composer or vCenter server in the 5-30 minute range as logins and access to the View environment are not immediately affected by View Composer downtime. System administrators should be aware that this situation can eventually cause a login outage. If desktops are configured to refresh or recompose after a logoff, in the absence of a functional View Composer, the pool of desktops will eventually be exhausted. Users will not be able to start new sessions when the pool of available desktops is exhausted.

For View environments with dedicated desktops, it is possible to operate without the View Composer for days as it is very rare to require Recompose or Refresh operations.

First, we determine whether we are going to install the View Composer on a dedicated machine or on the vCenter.

The View Composer currently can only be installed on a Windows 2008 R2 or higher version server. If you are using a vCenter appliance, you cannot install the View Composer on that appliance and you will require a separate Window Server VM for the View Composer.

When vCenter is installed on a Windows server, the View Composer can be co-installed on that server. In practice, the performance requirements for the View Composer are much smaller than the vCenter Server. Since vCenter and the View Composer have similar High Availability requirements, in practice co-location should be considered best practice unless dealing with a very large View environment.

Co-locating the View Composer with vCenter considerations

If we install the View Composer on the vCenter, we only need to worry about keeping the vCenter VM and database up and running. With shared storage, we can utilize VMware High Availability to restart the vCenter and View Composer server in the event of a host failure. This solution is acceptable for smaller View environments where the vCenter is not needed 100 percent of the time, or licensing costs are a significant consideration.

In the event of leveraging only the local storage, we can use the VMware Replication Appliance to replicate the vCenter to another host. The Replication Appliance has the downside of requiring manual intervention for restarting the vCenter on the backup host. It also can potentially mean some data loss on the database in the event of a failure and potentially a call to VMware to resolve any database issues. We can also utilize a backup solution, such as VMware Data Protection or various third-party solutions, and simply restore the VM from backup. This will be much slower than the replication method described previously.

Our other alternative is to install the View Composer and vCenter database on a highly available database cluster. This requires vCenter 5.5 or higher to support Microsoft SQL clusters or Oracle clusters. This has the upside of not losing data in the event of a failure but requires careful planning to ensure that there are not two instances of the vCenter or View Composer services running. We can choose to either run two vCenter/View Composer servers using a third-party Application Cluster software in an Active/Backup scenario or we can repeat the Replication Appliance scenario and simply have a cold backup vCenter / View Composer VM ready on our second node. VMware currently supports using Microsoft Cluster Services to provide High Availability for the vCenter. You can utilize solutions from the following vendors using their documentation on the process:

- MSCS (Microsoft Cluster Services)
- Microsoft SQL Server 2012 or 2014 AlwaysOn
- Oracle Real Application Clusters (RAC)
- VCS (Veritas Cluster Services)
- Symantec ApplicationHA

 Check out the following VMware knowledge base article for more details: http://kb.vmware.com/selfservice/microsites/search. do?language=en_US&cmd=displayKC&externalId=1024051.

Installation of the View Composer 6.0

VMware Horizon View requires a working ESXi and a vCenter server. You will need the following to continue:

- FQDN or IP address of the vCenter server
- Login information for the vCenter server with local administration rights

- Download the most current versions of the following software from `http://my.vmware.com`:

    ° Horizon View Connection Server (x64)

    ° Horizon View Composer

    ° Horizon View Agent (64-bit) or Horizon View Agent (32-bit) to match your guest OS

- One Windows server (Version 2008 R2 or higher) or an existing Windows vCenter server

- Ensure each Windows server is joined to the Active Directory domain

- OCDB connection setup for the View Composer with credentials that have full access to the database

> For compatibility concerns, please consult the VMware Product Interoperability Matrix:
>
> `http://partnerweb.vmware.com/comp_guide2/sim/interop_matrix.php`

The following steps outline how to install the View Composer:

1. Launch the View Composer installer on the Windows server that we are installing. This can be either a Windows vCenter server or a standalone Windows server.

2. On the **Welcome to the Installation Wizard for VMware Horizon View Composer** window, hit **Next**.

3. On the **License Agreement** window, select **I accept the terms in the license agreement** and hit **Next**.

4. Select the installation location using the **Change...** button and hit **Next**.

5. Type in the name of the ODBC Data Source Name (DSN). Type in the username for the database. Type in the password for the database connection and hit **Next**.

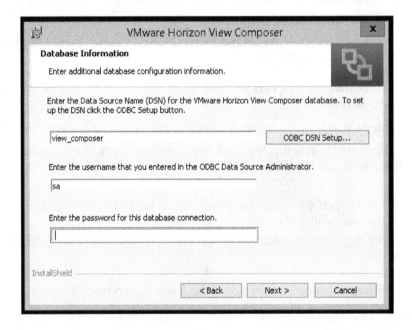

6. Leave the default SOAP Port as **18443**. Select **Create default SSL certificate**.

7. On the **Read to Install the Program** window, select **Install**.

8. On the **Installer Completed** window, hit **Finish**.

9. You will be required to restart the Windows server the View Composer is installed on. Hit **Yes** to restart the server.

We completed the installation of the View Composer. We can now move onto the installation of the View Connection servers.

Functions of the View Connection servers

The View Connection servers form the core of the View environment. They manage the following tasks:

- **Administration Interface**: The View Composer hosts the Administration Interface for systems administration access. Both the first View Connection server and any replica View Connection servers will host an administration interface. The administrative interface can be accessed via the URL `https://<View Connection Server FQDN>/admin`.

- **Entitlement Management**: The View Connection server manages the permissions that each user has to each desktop. It also manages the long-term assignments of dedicated desktops or full-clone desktops. Entitlements are stored in the local ADAM database.

- **Creation of full-cloned desktops** A full clone is a copy of a VM that is independent of the parent VM. Changes to a full clone are separate from the parent VM.

  The View Connection server will issue commands to the View Composer to manage the full-cloned desktops. This includes storing information about the current state of the full-cloned desktop and monitoring the virtual desktop agent's status.

- **Creation of link-cloned desktops**: A link-cloned desktop is a copy of a VM that shares virtual disks with the parent VM in an ongoing manner. Changes can be made to the parent VM and imaged over the rest of the link-cloned desktops. Link-cloned desktops share storage in a space-efficient manner that greatly reduces storage size requirements.

The View Connection server will issue commands to the View Composer to manage the link-cloned desktops. This includes storing information about the current state of the linked clone and monitoring the virtual desktop's agent status during a recompose, refresh, or rebalance action. The View Connection server monitors the quantity of desktops, both available and in use. Based on the provisioning requirements set on the link-cloned pool, it will allocate additional desktops to meet demand.

- **Agent/Client session broker**: The View Connection server is responsible for setting up sessions between clients (client application, thin clients, zero client, and so on) and the virtual desktop agents. It manages a list of entitlements for each View pool and will assign appropriate desktops to the user when they log in.

- **View HTML access**: When installed, HTML access permits users to log into their virtual desktops using a common web browser. This allows users to quickly access virtual desktop resources without requiring local installation of the View agent.

- **ADAM Replication**: The majority of View Connection server's configuration and state information is stored in an ADAM database. View Connection servers will replicate this data between each other continuously to maintain a consistent state across a cluster of View Connection servers.

Installation of View Connection Server 6.0

To install VMware View Connection servers, here are the prerequisites:

- A dedicated service account with Domain Administrator privileges for VMware Horizon View or a service account with the following permissions:
    - List Contents
    - Read All Properties
    - Write All Properties
    - Read Permissions
    - Reset Password
    - Create Computer Objects
    - Delete Computer Objects

- FQDN or IP address of the vCenter server.

- Login information for the vCenter server with local administration rights.
- Download the following from `http://my.vmware.com`:
    - Horizon View Connection Server (x64)
    - Horizon View Composer
    - Horizon View Agent (64-bit) or Horizon View Agent (32-bit) to match your guest OS
- Two Windows servers, version 2008 R2 or higher.
- The Windows firewall should be turned on for the View Connection server; the View Connection server will automatically add the required firewall rules as part of the installation.
- Each Windows server should be joined to Active Directory.
- FQDN names of the Horizon View Connection servers.
- A shared FQDN name for both Horizon View Connection servers with DNS load balancing.
- A certificate trusted by the clients, with the DNS names of both Horizon View Connection servers and the shared FQDN.
- A web browser with the latest version of Adobe flash player installed.
- OCDB connection setup for the View Event database, along with credentials.
- A license key for VMware Horizon View.

> For system requirements, please visit the VMware Documentation Center and verify the requirements against your environment:
>
> `https://pubs.vmware.com/horizon-61-view/index.jsp#com.vmware.horizon-view.installation.doc/GUID-E1B927CD-20A1-47B5-B613-BB9F1A4B58CB.html`

Installing the View Standard server

The following steps need to be performed:

1. Launch the VMware Horizon View Connection Server installer.
2. On the page that says **Welcome to the Installation Wizard for VMware Horizon View Connection Server**, hit **Next**.
3. On the license agreement page, select **I accept the terms in the license agreement** and hit **Next**.

4. Select the installation path for the VMware Horizon View Connection server. You can use the **Change…** button to select the path. Hit the **Next** button.

5. Select **View Standard Server** and ensure **Install HTML Access** has been checked. Click on **Next**.

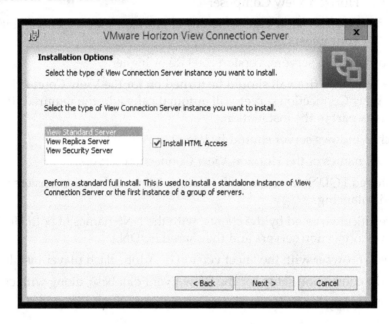

6. On the **Data Recovery** window, enter a data recovery password and then re-enter it. Select **Next** when finished.

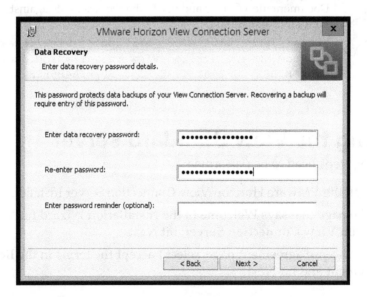

7. On the **Firewall Configuration** screen, select **Configure Windows Firewall automatically**. Click on **Next** to continue.

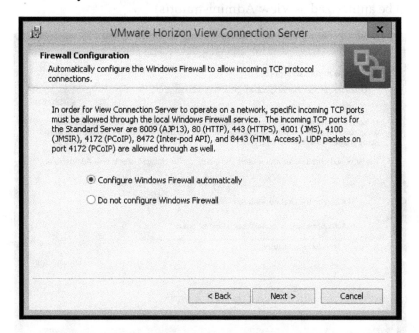

 Windows firewall should be left on for View Connection servers as it is required to communicate via IPsec with View Security servers.

8. On the **Initial View Administrators** screen, select **Authorize a specific domain user or domain group**. Enter the domain group or user that will be authorized as View Administrator(s).

9. On the **User Experience Improvement Program** screen, click on **Next**.
10. On the **Ready to Install the Program** window, click on **Install**.
11. On the **Installer Completed** window, click on **Finish**.

Installing the View Replica Server

Next, we will install the View Replica Server:

1. Launch the VMware Horizon View Connection Server installer.
2. On the page that says **Welcome to the Installation Wizard for VMware Horizon View Connection Server**, hit **Next**.
3. On the license agreement page, select **I accept the terms in the license agreement** and hit **Next**.
4. Select the installation path for the VMware Horizon View Connection server. You can use the **Change...** button to select the path. Click on the **Next** button.
5. On the **Installation Options** window, select **View Replica Server** and ensure **Install HTML Access** is selected. Click on **Next**.

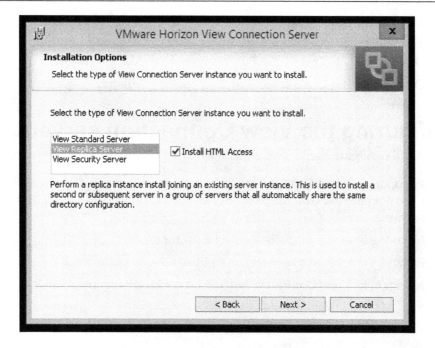

6. On the **Source Server** window, type the full FQDN path of the initial View Connection server. Ensure that the replica server can directly communicate with the original View Connection server.

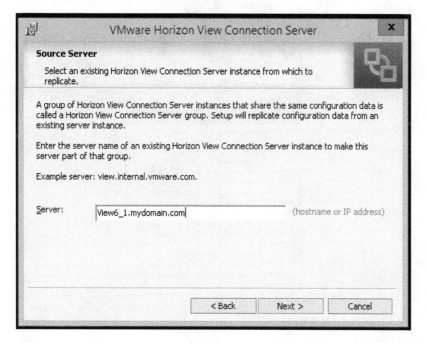

7. On the **Firewall Configuration** screen, select **Configure Windows Firewall automatically**. Hit **Next** to continue.

8. On the **Ready to Install the Program** window, click on **Install**.

9. On the **Installer Completed** window, click on **Finish**.

Configuring the View Connection servers

Next, we will configure the View Connection servers for use with our environment:

1. We open up a web browser to our View Connection Server administration page `https://<fqdn of view connection server 1>/admin` (for example, `https://view6_1.mydomain.com/admin`).

2. Next, log in using your View Administrator credentials.

3. Expand the inventory tree on the right-hand side of the window.

4. Navigate to **View Configuration | Product Licensing and Usage**.

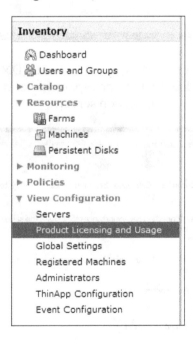

5. Select **Edit License...** and enter a valid VMware Horizon View license.

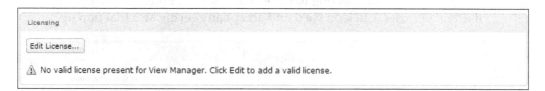

6. Navigate to **View Configuration | Servers**.

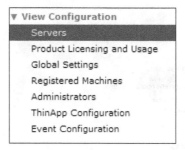

7. Select the **vCenter Servers** tab and hit **Add...**.

8. Enter the FQDN of the vCenter as value for the **Server address** field. Enter the username for connecting to the vCenter server. Enter the password for the vCenter user. Click on **Next** and accept any certificates that pop up.

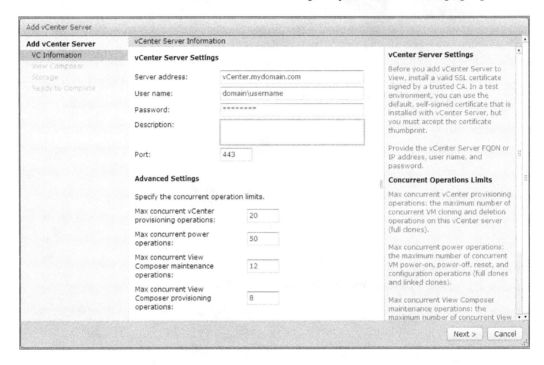

9. Enter the details about your View Composer and hit **Next**. Accept any certificates that pop up.

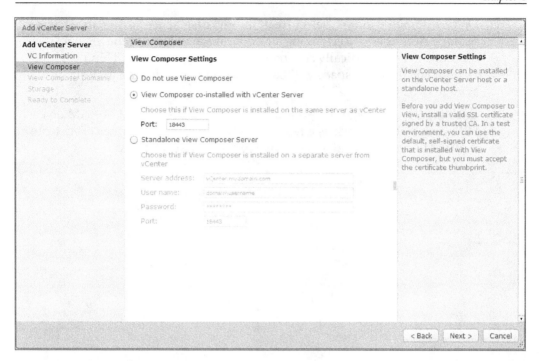

10. Add the domain(s) that View virtual desktops will be joined to. Click on **Next**.

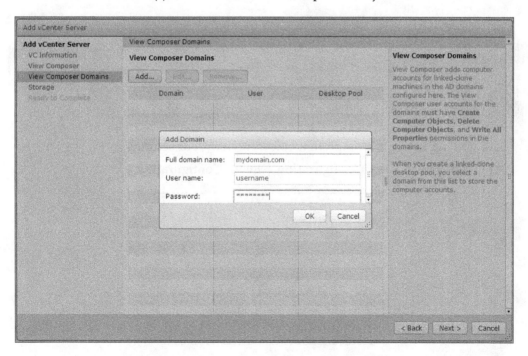

11. On the **Storage** window, select **Reclaim VM disk space** and **Enable View Storage Accelerator**. Reclaiming VM disk space will cause the virtual desktops to be periodically scanned for empty space. Using Thin Provision technology, the extra space will be periodically freed for the underlying storage to use.

Enabling View Storage Accelerator allocates a small amount of RAM on each ESXi host that will work as a read cache for the virtual desktops. The default is 1024 MB and is considered optimal in most cases. Hit **Next**.

12. On the **Ready to Complete** window, review your settings and select **Finish**.

13. Navigate to **View Configuration | Event Configuration**.

14. Select **Edit...** and enter the details for **Event Database**.

We have now configured two View Connection servers in a redundant pair. The ADAM database stored on each View Connection server will now automatically replicate any changes made to the rest of the cluster.

Network services HA

Now that we have functional View Connection servers, we must now finish the environment setup to ensure High Availability.

Configuring DNS

Our first task is to set up a DNS round robin. In this scenario, we are going to configure a DNS entry for each View Connection server and then a shared DNS entry for DNS load balancing. We also need to install a certificate on both View Connection servers that match the DNS entries we will be using.

Configure the following on the DNS server:

- A record with the FQDN of the 1st View Connection server with the first server's IP
- A record with the FQDN of the 2nd View Connection server with the second server's IP
- A record with the shared FQDN with the first View Connection server's IP
- A record with the shared FQDN with the second View Connection server's IP

After this is set up, all View clients should be configured to use the shared FQDN. The client will automatically switch View Connection servers in the event of an outage. Note that the outage will still cause a client to disconnect in most cases.

For more information on configuring DNS round robin on Microsoft DNS servers, visit https://technet.microsoft.com/en-us/library/cc787484%28v=ws.10%29.aspx.

Configuring certificates for the View Connection servers

Once DNS is set up, we can move ahead and configure the certificates on the View Connection servers. We can set up the certificates in one of the following manners:

- Configure two certificates, each certificate with the FQDN of the individual Connection server and the shared FQDN. Each server gets its own certificate.

- Configure one certificate. This certificate is installed on each View Connection server and has the FQDN of each View Connection server and the shared FQDN.

- Use a wildcard certificate. This certificate is configured to have the wildcard of the parent domain of the View Connection servers.

For each method used, install the certificate in the Computer Certificate Store of each of the View Connection servers. Make sure to set the friendly name of the certificate to vdm. Once the certificate is installed, restart the View Connection server and HTML Access services. You can verify that the certificate is correctly installed by navigating a web browser to the Administration Interface of each View Connection server. The certificate presented to the web browser should match the one installed.

For more information on certificate installation, refer to the VMware documentation at https://pubs.vmware.com/horizon-view-60/ index.jsp#com.vmware.horizon-view.certificates.doc/ GUID-DC255880-8AB2-45BF-93D9-14942DBE13AB.html

Configuring VMware vCenter High Availability & DRS rules

Once all our services are in place, we need to configure vCenter to run our systems in a High Availability aware manner. Note that for systems that are configured only with local storage, we can skip these steps; High Availability and DRS don't apply to systems that only have local storage.

We will configure the following in the next steps:

- VMware HA
- VMware DRS and DRS rules

We will now walk through the steps to configure vCenter:

1. Log into the VMware vSphere Web Client. The Web Client can be found at `https://<FQDN of vCenter>:9443`.

2. Navigate to **Home | vCenter | Inventory Lists | Clusters**.

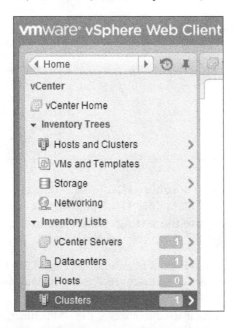

3. Navigate to the cluster where the View servers are installed.

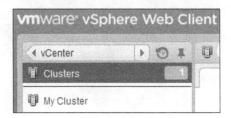

4. Go to **Actions | Settings**.

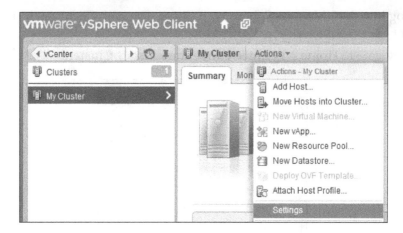

5. Navigate to **Services | vSphere HA**. Ensure that **Host Monitoring, VM Monitoring,** and **Datastore Heartbeating** are configured. Use the **Edit** button to configure the settings if they are not configured.

Host monitoring is used to monitor physical ESXi host crashes and faults. The fault can be discovered using various methods such as datastore heartbeating or network pinging.

VM monitoring is used to check if the VM is functional. This can be used to monitor the Windows server and Windows client OS VMs that are being used with the View.

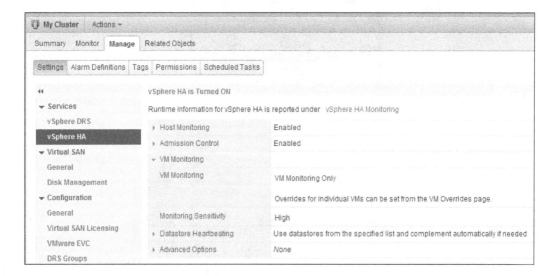

6. Navigate to **Services | vSphere DRS**. Ensure vSphere DRS is turned **ON**. If DRS is off, you can turn DRS on using the **Edit** button.

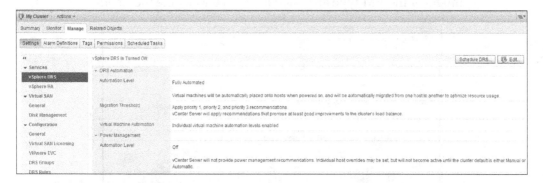

7. Navigate to **Services | DRS Rules**. Here, we will configure a DRS rule to separate the following VMs (one rule per VM type):

   ° View Connection servers
   ° Domain controllers
   ° DNS servers
   ° Clustered SQL servers
   ° DHCP servers
   ° vCenter active and backup servers
   ° View Composer active and backup servers

8. Under **DRS Rules**, select **Add**. Add the servers of the individual VM type (View Connection server, domain controller, DNS, and so on) Ensure the members of the VM type are listed as Virtual Machine members.

 Check out the VMware documentation on DRS for more information: `https://pubs.vmware.com/vsphere-55/index.jsp#com.vmware.vsphere.resmgmt.doc/GUID-FF28F29C-8B67-4EFF-A2EF-63B3537E6934.html`

Configuring VM startup/shutdown rules

For hosts that only have local storage, having properly configured startup and shutdown rules is essential as there is no way to migrate VMs off the host during the event of a power failure or host failure. You should configure the host so as to power on the VMs with local storage to ensure that they re-join the cluster. Note that while ESXi clusters with High Availability and shared storage make this step optional, it is best practice to have this configured anyway.

We will configure the VM startup/shutdown rules for the hosts now:

1. Navigate to the host where you will be configuring the VM startup/shutdown rules.

2. Select the **Manage** tab on the host.

3. Go to **Virtual Machines | VM Startup/Shutdown**.

4. Hit the **Edit...** button.

5. Configure the VMs to start up automatically in the following order:
   - DNS servers
   - DHCP servers
   - Domain controllers
   - SQL Cluster servers
   - vCenter servers
   - View Composer
   - Any applicable vShield components
   - Applicable file storage servers for any View profiles or user data
   - View Connection servers
   - All other servers

6. Leave the virtual desktops to start up manually; the View Connection server will power on virtual desktops as needed.

Failure testing checklist

Every good cluster should be failure-ready. As part of testing, I've provided a checklist to run through in order to verify the configuration and good standing of any View High Availability environment.

These steps should be performed in a test environment, and checked against the production environment. Periodic maintenance windows in the production environment can be carried out to test the failure scenarios and validate the environment.

Note that the loss of a View Connection server will disconnect any connected sessions, but the View client should be able to restart the session on the other View Connection server after it reconnects.

Run through each step and verify that VMware Horizon View is still working and can service new logins:

1. Power off each host, one at a time.
2. Power off each View Connection server, one at a time.
3. Power off each SQL Cluster server, one at a time.
4. Power off the View Composer server and start it on another host.
5. Power off the vCenter server and start it on another host.
6. Check whether any applicable vSphere replication is working.
7. Check whether each ESXi host is configured to power on after a power loss.
8. Check whether the VM startup/shutdown on each ESXi host is being followed and successfully starts VMs after a power failure.
9. Check whether VMware High Availability migrates VMs onto another host after a host failure.
10. Check that VMware DRS doesn't place VMs of the same type on the same host.
11. Check whether the DNS round robin is working via `nslookup`.
12. Document View High Availability procedures.
13. Train other systems administrators about View High Availability procedures.

Take a break. Your VMware Horizon View servers are walk-away safe.

Summary

In this chapter, we successfully configured and deployed VMware View in a highly available cluster. We covered software requirements, network requirements, and hardware requirements. We also discussed the topologies available to us to deploy highly available services.

In the next chapter, we will talk about the VMware View Security servers and how we can configure them in a High Availability environment.

2

VMware View 6.0 Security Server HA

In this chapter, we will discuss the functions and installation of the View Security server. We will cover the installation of a dual security server setup to provide redundancy in the event of a failure. We will also cover the firewall and DNS settings required for the View Security servers and general guidelines for HA planning.

In this chapter, we will cover the following topics:

- Functions of the View Security server
- Firewall and DNS requirements of the View Security server
- High Availability planning for the View Security server
- Installation of the View Security server
- View Security server failure checklist

Functions of the View Security server

The VMware Horizon View Security server acts as a bridge between external clients and the internal View Connection server. The security server provides the following features:

- **HTTP to HTTPS redirect**: The security server will send a redirect to HTTPS for any traffic that arrives over port 80.
- **HTTPS/Horizon View web page**: The security server provides a web page for client web browsers to connect to. It enables clients to authenticate with the server for HTML Access and provides a link to download the Windows, Mac OS X, and Linux clients.

- **HTML Access**: Enables clients to log into remote desktops via their web browser using only the HTTP/HTTPS protocol. This allows all HTML5 compatible web browsers to access View Horizon desktops. This includes various mobile browsers, such as the Apple Safari on iOS and Android-based web browsers.

- **IPsec encryption**: The security server will encrypt all traffic between the security server and connection server using IPsec. This ensures secure and reliable communication through the firewall. IPsec negotiates encryption and verifies the identities of the machines at both ends. It then encapsulates all designated IP traffic between the two machines, ensuring that it cannot be decrypted or altered by a third-party attacker. IPsec has the additional benefit of reducing the number of ports that need to be allowed through the firewall.

- **PCoIP and USB redirection**: The security server acts as a bridge between the external clients and the remote desktops, allowing video, audio, and USB redirection to function on external clients. PCoIP provides faster response times and lower bandwidth requirements than typical RDP sessions, making for a great remote desktop experience.

- **Security**: The security server provides an additional layer of protection for the connection servers. IPS and firewall rules can be placed between the connection server and the security server.

 For more details about the security server, read the VMware documentation at https://pubs.vmware.com/horizon-62-view/index.jsp#com.vmware.horizon-view.planning.doc/GUID-57D362EB-AC04-45B8-87AA-05A15A998211.html.

Firewall and DNS requirements of the View Security server

The View Security server should be set up in a DMZ-type environment with firewalls separating it from both the WAN and LAN traffic.

The following rules need to be configured on the firewalls:

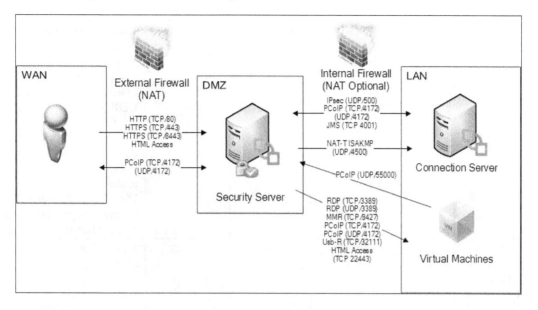

External ports used to communicate with clients are listed in the following table:

Source	Source port	Protocol	Destination	Destination port	Notes
Horizon client	TCP/Any	HTTP	Security server	TCP 80	For HTTP to HTTPS redirects.
Horizon client	TCP/Any	HTTPS	Security server	TCP 443	For HTTPS communication with the web browser and the View Horizon client.
Horizon client	TCP/Any UDP/Any	PCoIP	Security server	TCP 4172 UDP 4172	For communications between the View Horizon client and the security server. This port carries all the PCoIP traffic including USB tunneling, audio, and video.

Source	Source port	Protocol	Destination	Destination port	Notes
Security server	UDP 4172	PCoIP	Horizon client	UDP Any	The security servers send PCoIP data back to the client from UDP port 4172. The destination UDP port is the source port from the received UDP packets. These packets are in reply to the client data. Most firewalls won't require a separate rule for this traffic
Client web browser	TCP/Any	HTTPS	Security server	TCP 8443	This port is used for HTML Access traffic between the security server and the client's web browser

Internal ports used for communication with the View Connection server are listed here:

Source	Source port	Protocol	Destination	Destination port	Notes
Security server	UDP 500	IPsec	Connection server	UDP 500	The security server uses IPsec to encrypt communications to the connection server.
Connection server	UDP 500	IPsec	Security server	UDP 500	The connection server uses IPsec to encrypt the communications to the security server.
Security server	UDP 4500	NAT-T ISAKMP	Connection server	UDP 4500	Used in the event of a NAT firewall being used between the connection server and the security server.

Source	Source port	Protocol	Destination	Destination port	Notes
Connection server	TCP Any	AJP13	Connection server	TCP 8009	The security server connects to the View Connection server to forward web traffic from external client devices. It's not used when IPsec is used.
Security server	TCP Any	JMS	Connection server	TCP 4001	Java Message Services.
Security server	TCP Any	RDP	Remote desktop	TCP 3389	Remote desktop protocol traffic to the desktops.
Security server	TCP Any	MMR	Remote desktop	TCP 9427	Used for MMR traffic between the security server and the remote desktop.
Security server	TCP Any UDP 55000	PCoIP	Remote desktop or application	TCP 4172 UDP 4172	PCoIP traffic between the security server and connection server
Remote desktop or application	UDP 4172	PCoIP	Security server	UDP 55000	Remote desktop and application send data to the security server from UDP 4172. Most firewalls won't require a separate rule for this traffic, as it is the return path of the above traffic.
Security server	TCP Any	USB-R	Remote desktop	TCP 32111	USB redirection traffic between an external client and remote desktop.

Source	Source port	Protocol	Destination	Destination port	Notes
Security server	TCP Any	HTTPS	Remote desktop	TCP 22443	Used for HTML Access. The security server connects to the remote desktop on port 22443 to communicate with the Blast agent.
Security server		ESP	Connection server		Encapsulated AJP13 traffic when NAT traversal is required. ESP is IP protocol 50.
Connection server		ESP	Security server		Encapsulated AJP13 traffic when NAT traversal is required. ESP is IP protocol 50.

DNS requirements for the View Security server are as follows:

- An internal FQDN for each View Security server that is unique to that server
- A shared external FQDN for each cluster of View Security servers

High Availability planning for the View Security server

Each VMware View Horizon Security server is paired with a View Connection server. This relationship can be many-to-one (multiple View Security servers per connection server) or one-to-one (one security server connected to one connection server). Connection servers do not need a security server to function, but do require a security server to handle external clients and any NAT translation that is applicable.

The View Security servers don't have configuration data or management services that are required to keep the Horizon View environment running. The only prerequisite for rebuilding a View Security server is to have a functional View Connection server. Since the View Security servers don't talk to each other, there is no need for cluster logic beyond load balancing and failover. For most environments, DNS load balancing will be sufficient—assuming that the View Security servers have identical hardware. Note that DNS load balancing will allow clients to connect after a failure, but some clients may try the failed server first before trying a working server. Larger environments may still opt for hardware load balancing solutions that will gracefully failover clients to working servers. Load balancers will only handle the HTTPS and HTTP traffic. PCoIP bypasses the load balancer and communicates directly with the security server.

To create highly available View Security servers, we simply deploy and configure two or more security servers using DNS load balancing or a hardware/software load balancer. You should distribute the pairing of the security servers to different View Connection servers so as to reduce the possible loss of total environment in the event that one connection server is not available. In the event of a View Connection server failure, the paired View Security server(s) will stop functioning.

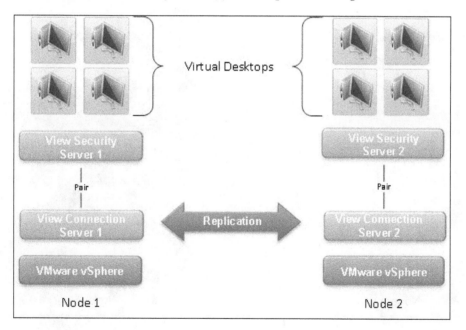

It is important that the View Security servers are hosted in such a way that the environment is not taken down in a single host failure. Monitoring the environment is key to responding to server failures. Generally, this is accomplished by monitoring the running services and HTTPs. Please refer to *Chapter 8, Monitoring VMware Horizon View*, for more details about View monitoring.

The next scenario depicts a Node 2 failure. Since View Security server 2 is paired to View Connection Server 2, View Security Server 2 can no longer service external View clients in the absence of View Connection Server 2. Since View Security Server 1 is hosted on the failed Node 2, View Connection Server 1 no longer has any security servers that can handle external View clients. In this scenario, a single host failure has prevented all external View clients from connecting to their desktops.

The simplest way to ensure that we don't lose our ability to service external clients is to ensure that the View Security servers are hosted on the same host as their paired View Connection server or on an entirely separate vSphere cluster. We should create DRS affinity rules for the View Connection servers and their paired View Security servers. In the case of local storage only, we install the View Security server on the same host as the paired View Connection server.

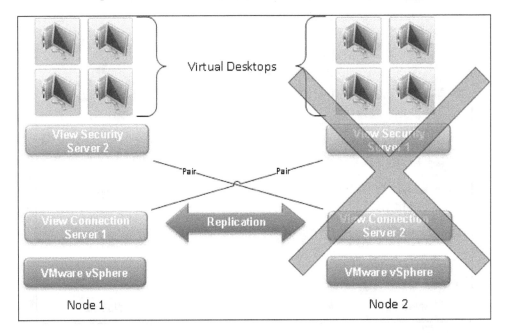

Installing the View Security server

Let's take a look at the various steps involved in installing a View Security server.

Prerequisites

The prerequisites for installation of the View Security servers are as follows:

- Two Windows servers running 2008 R2 or higher, 64-bit edition.

- Windows Updates turned on and automatically installed on the servers.

  Note that Windows updates may reboot the server at a scheduled time. Stagger the update times of the security servers to ensure that there is always one available. Hardware/software load balancers will be able to handle the outage automatically, but clients may be disconnected initially during the reboot.

  If this is not as per company policy, ensure the servers are regularly updated to mitigate security issues as they are discovered.

- Windows Firewall should be turned on for both the View Connection servers and the View Security servers

- The View Security servers should *not* be joined to Active Directory.

  Note that a part of the security and mitigation of attacks depends on the server not being part of the Active Directory domain, to reduce the privileges of any attacker who compromises the system. Group polices that are required should be applied manually.

  Management services such as Software Center Configuration Manager should be manually installed and configured.

- Static IPs should be assigned to all servers.

- Static external IPs should be assigned to both servers via NAT.

- NAT, firewall rules, and DNS should be configured as per the *Firewall and DNS requirements of the View Security server* section.

- Download the View Connection server executable from http://my.vmware.com.

- Credentials for the local administrator for the View Security server.

- Administrator credentials for the View Connection servers.

- Install the certificates for the View Security servers to use (see *Chapter 1, VMware Horizon View 6.0 Connection Server HA*, for reference).

For more information on certificate installation, refer to the VMware documentation at `https://pubs.vmware.com/horizon-view-60/index.jsp#com.vmware.horizon-view.certificates.doc/GUID-DC255880-8AB2-45BF-93D9-14942DBE13AB.html`.

Installation

Follow the steps given here to install the View Security server:

1. Launch the View Connection server executable on the server you intend to use as the View Security server.

2. On the **Welcome to the Installation Wizard for VMware Horizon View Connection Server** window, click on **Next**.

3. On the **License Agreement** window, select **I accept the terms in the license agreement** and click on **Next**.

4. On the **Destination Folder** window, use the **Change...** button to specify the installation location. Click on **Next**.

5. In the **Installation Options** window, select **View Security Server** and hit **Next**.

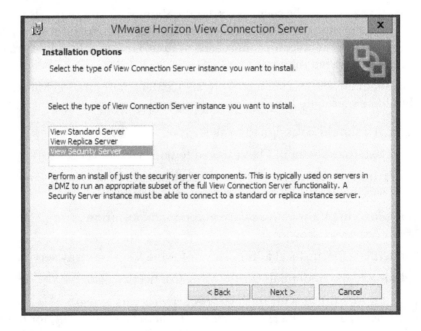

6. On the **Paired Horizon View Connection Server** window, type the full internal FQDN of the connection server you are going to pair with. Note that this is not the shared FQDN but that of the individual server. Then, click on **Next**.

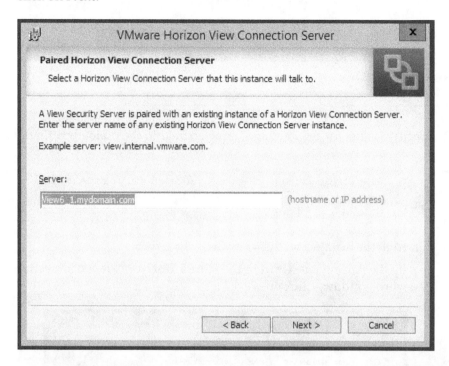

7. We will leave the installer on **Paired Horizon View Connection Server Password** and go to the View Connection server to specify the security server pairing password.

8. Log in to the View Connection server.

9. Navigate to **Inventory | View Configuration | Servers**.

10. Click on the **Connection Servers** tab.

11. Select the connection server you are going to pair the security server with. Go to **More Commands | Specify Security Server Pairing Password....**

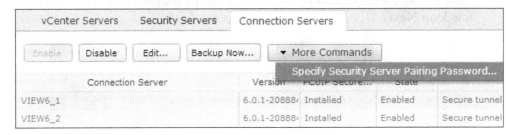

12. Specify a value for the **Pairing Password** field in the dialog box that pops up.

 Note that specified pairing passwords expire after a specified amount of time. The next steps will be time sensitive. The default timeout is 30 minutes.

13. Return to the installer on the View Security server.

14. Specify the pairing password in the **Paired Horizon View Connection Server Password** window. Click on **Next**.

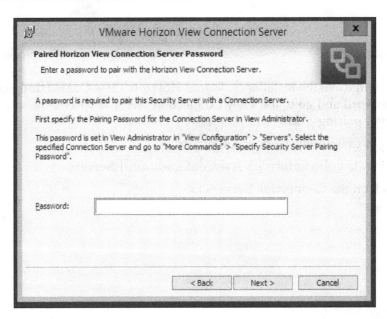

15. In the **View Security Server Configuration** window, specify the following attributes:

    ° **External URL**

    ° **PCoIP External URL**

    ° **Blast External URL**

16. On the **Firewall Configuration** window, select **Configure Windows Firewall automatically**. Click on **Next**

17. On the **Ready to Install the Program** window, select **Install**.

18. Reboot the server once the installation is finished.

19. Repeat steps 1-18 on the second View Security server using the second View Connection server for pairing.

HA DRS and power

Just like in *Chapter 1, VMware Horizon View 6.0 Connection Server HA*, we want to configure our ESXi hosts to handle our pair of View Security servers.

Two or more ESXi hosts with shared storage

In this example, we assume that the first View Connection server is paired with the first View Security server and that the second View Connection server is paired with the second View Security server. We want to ensure that the server pairs survive a single host failure.

For clusters with shared storage and three or less ESXi hosts, we want to configure the following DRS rules:

- A DRS VM Affinity rule to keep the first View Connection server and the first View Security server on the same host
- A DRS VM Affinity rule to keep the second View Connection server and the second View Security server on the same host
- A DRS VM Anti-affinity rule to keep the first View Security server and the second View Security server on different hosts

Four or more ESXi hosts with shared storage

For clusters with shared storage and four or more ESXi hosts, we have two choices to consider. We can separate all the VMs onto separate hosts and risk having one of the connection servers being lost. In this case, the paired security server would stop functioning, preventing some external sessions. We can use a load balancer to monitor both servers and offline the non-functional security server in the event of a connection server failure. Having the View servers on separate hosts would maximize CPU power available to View servers. This configuration would also increase intercluster network traffic due to the View Security server and View Connection server being on separate hosts. Configure the following DRS rule:

A DRS VM Anti-affinity rule to keep the first View Security server, the second View Security server, the first View Connection server, and the second View Connection server on different hosts.

The alternative scenario is to configure the VMs with the same DRS rules as the three ESXi servers or less scenario. This would ensure that failover always occurs successfully in the event of a host failure. This scenario is recommended for DNS load balancing. Configure the following DRS rule:

- A DRS VM Affinity rule to keep the first View Connection server and the first View Security server on the same host
- A DRS VM Affinity rule to keep the second View Connection server and the second View Security server on the same host
- A DRS VM Anti-affinity rule to keep the first View Security server and the second View Security server on different hosts

Two or more ESXi hosts with local storage

For clusters with local-only storage and three or less ESXi hosts, we want to install the View Security server and the paired View Connection server on the same host.

Four or more ESXi hosts with local storage

For clusters with local-only storage and four or more ESXi hosts, we have a choice to make. We can install the View Security servers and the View Connection servers all on separate hosts. The risk of this is having one of the connection servers being lost. In this case, the paired security server would stop functioning, preventing some external sessions. We can use a load balancer to monitor both servers and offline the non-functional security server in the event of a connection server failure. Having the View servers on separate hosts would maximize the CPU power available to the View servers. This configuration would also increase intercluster network traffic due to the View Security server and View Connection server being on separate hosts. This is recommended for environments with load balancers.

The alternative is to follow the same scenario as the two or more ESXi hosts and install the paired security server with the connection server. This is recommended for DNS load balancing.

Power on

Automatic power on should be configured on each host to power on the following services in this order:

- Any storage VMs (Network Attached Storage)
- Any security VMs (vShield, endpoints, and so on)
- Active Directory domain controllers

- vCenter server
- Any Storage VMs (Windows file sharing)
- Any load balancers
- View Connection servers
- View Security servers

View Security server failure checklist

Now, we will move onto failure testing for the View Security servers.

It's recommended that this failure checklist be carried out in a test environment prior to the environment being put into production. Ensure that the environment has adequate backups prior to testing.

Note that the loss of a View Security server will disconnect any connected sessions, but the View client should be able to restart the session on the other View Security server after it reconnects.

Run through each step and verify that VMware Horizon View is still working and can service new logins for external clients:

1. Power off each host, one at a time. Determine if the Power On rules and DRS rules function and if the environment has enough failure capacity to run without a server.

2. Power off each View Security server, one at a time. Determine if failover occurs successfully.

3. Check whether each ESXi host is configured to power on after a power loss.

4. Check whether the VM startup/shutdown on each ESXi host is being followed and successfully starts VMs after a power failure.

5. Check whether VMware HA migrates VMs onto another host after a host failure.

6. Check whether VMware DRS doesn't place VMs of the same type on the same host.

7. Check whether the DNS round robin is working via `nslookup`.

8. Document View HA procedures.

9. Train other systems administrators about View HA procedures.

Take a break. Your VMware Horizon View servers are safe.

Summary

In this chapter, we covered the installation and HA planning for the View Security server. We examined common failure modes for the View Security servers and pitfalls that need to be avoided. We covered DRS, HA, power rules, and various other considerations.

In the next chapter, we will cover load balancing and deployment planning for both the View Connection server and the View Security server.

3
Load Balancers and Deployment Planning

In this chapter, we will go over the network and topological requirements for a load balancer and networking for VMware Horizon View. We will cover each available load balancing method and the pros and cons of each. We will also discuss the ports used, the unique requirements of each port, and the DNS requirements.

In this chapter, we will cover the following topics:

- Ports used for load balancing
- DNS load balancing
- Windows Network Load Balancing
- Software or hardware load balancing
- View failure checklist

Ports used for load balancing

We covered the ports used for inter-server communication in *Chapter 2, VMware View 6.0 Security Server HA*. Here, we will cover the purpose and the requirements of the ports for load balancing. Your load balancer must be configured to load balance the following ports:

- **TCP Port 80 (HTTP)**: This is used to serve traffic to client web browsers for issuing a redirect to HTTPS. This port doesn't have any load balancing requirements. We can close this port or direct this port to a normal web server to issue the HTTPS redirect.

- **TCP Port 443 (HTTPS)**: This is used by clients for communicating and downloading information from the View Security Server. Clients can use HTTPS to set up a PCoIP session or to access the initial login screen for HTML access. It also provides links to the View Client downloads hosted on http://vmware.com.

  All clients must continue talking to the server they were initially served by. This can be accomplished by injecting a load balancer cookie into the HTTPS session (requires the load balancer to have the server certificate) or by doing client IP hashing/affinity.

- **TCP/UDP Port 4172 (PCoIP)**: This is used for PCoIP traffic. This includes Audio/Video and USB inputs. There are two options for PCoIP. We can configure the PCoIP traffic to bypass the load balancer and go directly to the security or connection servers. We can also configure the load balancer to act as the relay for these ports. The PCoIP ports must direct the client to the same server that the client was directed to for HTTPS. We should ensure that our load balancer is configured to have client persistence across all three port groups.

- **TCP Port 8443 (HTTPS/Blast)**: This is used for HTML access to the view servers. Clients will use this port to access View desktops from their web browsers. All clients must continue talking to the server they were initially served by. This can be accomplished by injecting a load balancer cookie into the HTTPS session (requires the load balancer to have the server certificate) or by doing client IP hashing/affinity.

- **TCP Port 32111 (USB Redirection)**: This is used for sending USB traffic between the client and the virtual desktop. This allows devices such as USB drives, microphones, speakers, and VoIP phones to pass information back and forth with the virtual desktop. If USB redirection is allowed, this port needs to be made available via the load balancer.

DNS load balancing

In the previous chapters, we set up the View Horizon servers with basic DNS load balancing. DNS load balancing involves setting multiple host (A/AAAA) records for the DNS entry of the View connection servers and/or View Security servers. The DNS server with balancing provides multiple IP addresses per DNS entry to the View Horizon clients. The DNS server will randomly alternate between IP addresses served to the client to ensure multiple clients use different View Horizon servers. This provides basic load switching but doesn't account for balance. In practice (assuming identical hardware for the View servers), this will provide a load that is close to balanced but not quite. In the event of a View server failure, clients will timeout connecting to the failed server and try another IP. This method doesn't have a built-in method of monitoring uptime for services. In addition, DNS load balancing doesn't respond quickly to changes. If the TTL for the DNS record is long, it is possible an outage may be prolonged by bad cached DNS entries.

DNS load balancing offers the following advantages:

- It's easy to configure. We simply add multiple host (A) records to our DNS entry for the security servers and/or connection servers.
- It's inexpensive, as we can use our existing DNS servers.

DNS load balancing has the following disadvantages:

- No load monitoring. Load is determined by client behavior.
- No server monitoring. DNS servers don't monitor hosts.
- Client side failover. Clients may attempt to use a failed server, delaying login.
- Cached IP addresses may prolong an outage.

Here's a typical deployment of a DNS load distribution:

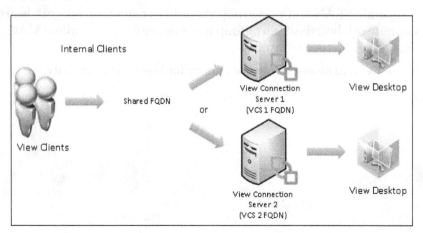

We insert two host (A/AAAA) records into our DNS for the shared FQDN of the two View Connection servers. We would then have a host (A/AAAA) record for each of the View Connection servers. When the client attempts to connect to the shared FQDN, it receives both of the View Connection server IPs. It will then choose a server to connect to.

Windows Network Load Balancing

Windows Network Load Balancing comes built-in with Windows Server 2008 R2, 2012, and 2012 R2. This allows two or more Windows servers to participate in a load balanced cluster. This cluster requires heartbeating between nodes to check for uptime and connectivity. The NLB works by sharing a virtual IP between hosts; this requires changing or spoofing the MAC address for the cluster IP. All hosts must have static IPs.

Windows Network Load Balancing offers the following advantages:

- Windows load balancing is supported and included in Windows 2008 R2, 2012, and 2012 R2, which means that the Security and Connection servers should already be licensed to use it.
- It supports up to 32 servers in a load balanced cluster.
- Servers can be added or removed on the fly. Note that clients connected to a removed server will get disconnected.
- Server failures are detected and traffic is rerouted.
- Load can be distributed via weighted average.

Windows Network Load Balancing has the following disadvantages:

- Complicated setup and configuration.
- A separate VLAN and port group should be created for network heartbeats. The network heartbeat port group must be configured to allow MAC address changes and forged transmits.
- It's not service aware. It can only check for layer 3 connectivity.

Here's a typical deployment of a Windows load balancer:

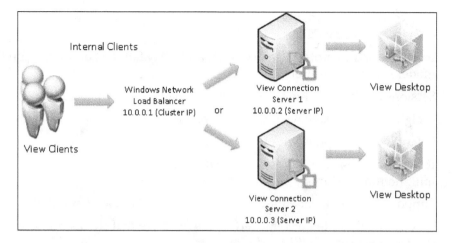

Here, the View clients will attempt to connect to the Windows cluster IP, which is shared between the two servers. The cluster IP is monitored by both View Connection servers, and the servers decide which will connect to the View client. This allows the servers to decide the load and compensate for failed members.

Software or hardware load balancing

Load balancers provide the highest amount of scalability and reliability of any solutions currently present. The load balancer is designed to handle all aspects of high availability operation to ensure the maximum uptime of a VMware Horizon View environment. To implement high availability with a hardware or software load balancer, the load balancer should be deployed in a high availability pair to guard against a load balancer outage. This can add two to four VMs or appliances to the View Environment and may significantly increase costs.

Note that when deploying software load balancer VMs it is necessary to configure appropriate anti-affinity DRS rules and to include the load balancer in the power on rules for each host.

Consult your load balancer vendor's documentation for appropriate configurations with VMware Horizon View. Your vendor will recommend best practices that reflect the features available to your load balancer.

The advantages of software or hardware load balancing are as follows:

- Service awareness, that is, the load balancer can probe and react to service outages, including PCoIP HTTPS
- It can be used to protect against WAN and LAN failures, depending on the model and configuration
- Sessions can be preserved in the case of a load balancer failure
- Weighted load balancing and proper load monitoring as well as metrics
- SSL offload is possible with load balancers
- It can offer firewall features such as DDoS, IPS, VPN, and multihoming features
- Supported servers, depending on the model and hardware selected
- Servers can be added or removed on the fly. Note that clients connected to a removed server will get disconnected

The disadvantages of software or hardware load balancing are as follows:

- Potentially very expensive when purchasing dedicated hardware solutions
- Requires two to four additional VMs or appliances to support end-to-end High Availability
- Configuration can be complicated

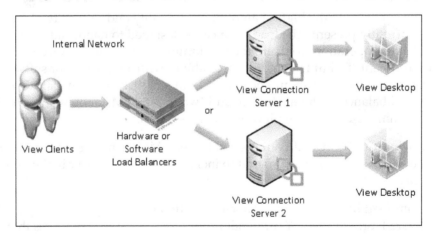

Here, the View clients connect to the hardware or software load balancer. The load balancer determines which server the client traffic will be directed to. The load balancer is responsible for monitoring the server load and checks for server failures. Once the client connects to the View connection server via HTTPS, the server will handle the return PCoIP traffic directly.

High Availability and failure planning

For implementing load balancers in the View Environment, there are many factors you need to consider before selecting a topology:

- Do we have external clients?
- Do we have internal clients?
- Are we going to do SSL offload?
- Is HTML Access enabled?
- What is our recovery time?
- How will we perform network maintenance?
- Do we need to use a secure gateway/tunnel for PCoIP traffic?
- What is our budget? Which solution can we implement with the hardware we have?
- How many clients do we need to support?

Let's examine the result of outages with various load balancing solutions and configurations. We will examine the topology diagrams for each scenario and how clients will be affected by each outage that may occur.

DNS round robin with internal-only clients

Let's examine the server setup and the consequences of high availability and failures. We will examine each probable event that can happen to a cluster and review the consequences of each event.

Consider each scenario in the image in the *DNS load balancing* section and how you choose to deal with it. Remember to document your decisions and train your staff on how to handle outages.

Event	Secure gateway/tunnel enabled	Secure gateway/tunnel disabled
View connection server 1 failure	Clients connected to View connection server 1 disconnect. Clients can reconnect on View connection server 2. New logins handled by View connection server 2. Some login delay may occur if the client first tries View connection server 1 for login.	Client sessions unaffected. New logins handled by View connection server 2. Some login delay may occur if the client first tries View connection server 1 for login.

Event	Secure gateway/tunnel enabled	Secure gateway/tunnel disabled
View connection server 2 failure	Clients connected to View connection server 2 disconnect. Clients can reconnect on View connection server 1. New logins handled by View connection server 1. Some login delay may occur if the client first tries View connection server 2 for login.	Client sessions unaffected. New logins handled by View connection server 1. Some login delay may occur if the client first tries View connection server 2 for login.
View connection server removed from DNS	The server removed from DNS will no longer handle new clients after the DNS TTL expires. New clients can still connect to the removed View connection server before the TTL has expired.	
View connection server added to DNS	The new connection server can start handling clients immediately. Clients cannot use the new connection server until the DNS TTL has expired.	
Maintenance required on the View connection server	The maintainer can remove the server from DNS and wait for all the clients to finish their sessions. Otherwise, the maintainer must wait for a maintenance window. Clients will be disconnected when the server is shutdown/removed from production.	The maintainer can remove the View connection server from DNS, wait for the DNS TTL to expire, and then begin maintenance.

Windows load balancing with internal-only clients

Let's examine the failure scenarios in a Windows load balancer environment. Each event depicts a probable failure event that may occur in the environment.

For reference, you can look at the image in the *Windows Network Load Balancing* section.

This should help guide administrators on what failures can be expected and how the environment can be configured:

Event	Secure gateway/tunnel enabled	Secure gateway/tunnel disabled
View connection server 1 failure	Clients connected to View connection server 1 disconnect. Clients can reconnect on View connection server 2. New logins handled by View connection server 2. No login delays.	Client sessions unaffected. New logins handled by View connection server 2. No login delays.
View connection server 2 failure	Clients connected to View connection server 2 disconnect. Clients can reconnect on View connection server 1. New logins handled by View connection server 1. No login delays.	Client sessions unaffected. New logins handled by View connection server 1. No login delays.
View connection server removed from cluster	Clients will immediately use other View connection servers when logging in. Clients will be disconnected from the removed connection server.	Clients will immediately use other View connection servers when logging in.
View connection server added to cluster	Clients will immediately use the added View connection servers when logging in.	
Windows updates required on the View connection server	For Windows updates, the maintainer can utilize cluster-aware updating for Windows Server 2012 or 2012 R2. Clients connected to the updated server will be disconnected. No login time delays.	For Windows updates, the maintainer can utilize cluster-aware updating for Windows Server 2012 or 2012 R2. Clients will be unaffected. No login time delays.
Maintenance required on the View connection server	Maintainer puts the View connection server into pause via Windows clustering using the Drain Roles command. New clients will be directed to other servers. The maintainer must wait for existing sessions to disconnect or wait for a maintenance window.	Maintainer puts the View connection server into pause via Windows clustering using the Drain Roles command. New clients will be directed to other servers. Existing sessions are unaffected.

Scenarios in software or hardware load balancing

Let's examine the common failure scenarios in a software or hardware load balanced environment. Note that we also have to consider the failure of the load balancer when considering our outage events.

For reference, you can see the image in the section *Software or hardware load balancing*.

Load balancers must themselves be redundant.

Event	Secure gateway/tunnel enabled	Secure gateway/tunnel disabled
View connection server 1 failure	Clients connected to View connection server 1 disconnect. Clients can reconnect on View connection server 2. New logins handled by View connection server 2. No login delays	Client sessions unaffected. New logins handled by View connection server 2. No login delays.
View connection server 2 failure	Clients connected to View connection server 2 disconnect. Clients can reconnect on View connection server 1. New logins handled by View connection server 1. No login delays.	Client sessions unaffected. New logins handled by View connection server 1. No login delays.
View connection server removed from the load balancer	Clients will immediately use other View connection servers when logging in. Pending the load balancer configuration and capabilities, clients may or may not continue to use the removed server until their session ends.	Clients will immediately use other View connection servers when logging in.
View connection server added to the load balancer	Clients will immediately use the added View connection servers when logging in. The load balancer may redirect existing traffic to the new server, pending configuration.	Clients will immediately use the added View connection servers when logging in.

Maintenance required on the View connection server	Maintainer puts the View connection server into maintenance mode via the load balancer (if capable). New clients will be directed to other servers. The maintainer must wait for existing sessions to disconnect or wait for a maintenance window.	Maintainer puts the View connection server into maintenance mode via the load balancer (if capable). New clients will be directed to other servers. Existing sessions are unaffected.
Load balancer failure with HA pair	Clients will immediately begin to use the other load balancer. Existing sessions may or may not be disconnected depending on the load balancer features and failover speed.	Clients will immediately begin to use the other load balancer. Existing sessions will be preserved.
Load balancer failure without HA pair	Clients are unable to log in, and existing sessions will be disconnected.	Clients are unable to log in, and existing sessions will continue.

DNS round robin for View security servers with external clients

When dealing with View security servers, the connection servers must be configured with secure gateway/tunnel enabled in order to service external clients. This reduces our HA features since all external clients will get disconnected in the event of a server failure.

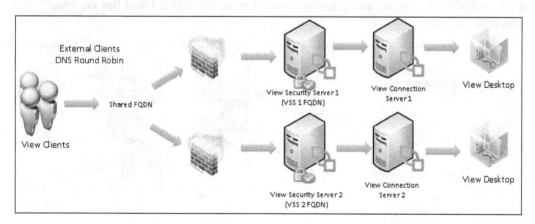

Event	Result
View Security Server failure	Clients will be disconnected and will use the other View Security Server to process a new login. Clients that connect to the failed Security Server first when logging in will experience delays.
View Connection Server failure	The View Security Server paired with the failed Connection Server will no longer be able to service logins. Clients will use the other Security Server for logins. Clients that connect to the failed Security Server first when logging in will experience delays.
View Security Server removed from DNS	The server removed from DNS will no longer handle new clients after the DNS TTL expires. New clients may still connect to the removed View Security Server before the TTL has expired.
View Security Server added to DNS	The new Security Server can start handling clients immediately. Clients may not use the new Security Server until the DNS TTL has expired.
Maintenance required on the View Security Server	The maintainer can remove the server from DNS and wait for all clients to finish their sessions. Otherwise, the maintainer must wait for a maintenance window. Clients will be disconnected when the server is shut down or removed from production.

Windows load balancing for View security servers with external clients

Windows load balancing for View security servers is somewhat different than the View connection servers scenario. The main difference is View security servers can't be joined to Active Directory, which means Windows Cluster Aware update isn't available. Again, secure gateway/tunnel must be enabled and has various HA consequences.

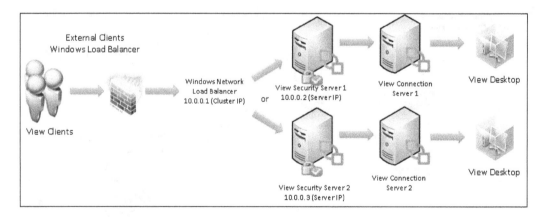

Event	Result
View security server failure	Clients will be disconnected and will use the other View security server to process a new login. No login delays as the other security server will take over the cluster IP.
View connection server failure	The View security server paired with the failed connection server will no longer be able to service logins. Windows clustering won't notice the failure of the View security server, since the cluster doesn't check service status. Clients might be rejected until they are sent to a different security server by chance.
View security server removed from cluster	The server removed from the cluster will no longer handle new clients. New clients will use the other security servers. Assuming the maintainer used the Pause > Drain Roles command, the server will continue to handle the existing clients until the session ends.
View security server added to DNS	The new security server can start handling clients immediately.
Maintenance required on the View security server	The maintainer can put the security server into Pause mode via Windows Clustering. Use the Pause > Drain Roles command to ensure a graceful shutdown. The security server will continue to handle the existing clients until the session ends.

Software or hardware load balancers for View security servers with external clients

Hardware load balancers share much of the same functionality as the above Windows Network Load Balancing scenario, with the exception that they can now handle the View connection server failure situation gracefully (thanks to service monitoring). Again, secure gateway/tunnel must be enabled and has various HA consequences.

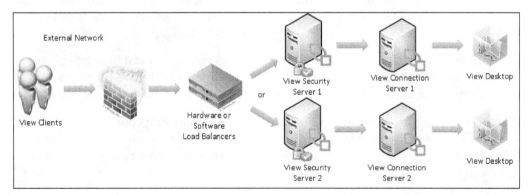

Event	Result
View security server failure	Clients will be disconnected and then use the other View security server to process a new login. No login delays as clients will automatically be redirected by the load balancer.
View connection server failure	The View security server paired with the failed connection server will no longer be able to service logins. The load balancer will notice the service outage and direct clients to the other security server.
View security server removed from cluster	The server removed from the cluster will no longer handle new clients. New clients will use the other security servers. Assuming the node was set to drain sessions, the existing client sessions will continue.
View security server added to DNS	The new security server can start handling clients immediately.
Maintenance required on the View security server	The maintainer can put the security server into maintenance mode and wait for all the existing sessions to terminate. The load balancer will allow existing sessions to continue.
Load balancer failure with HA pair	Clients will immediately begin to use the other load balancer. Existing sessions may or may not be disconnected depending on the load balancer features and failover speed.
Load balancer failure without HA pair	Clients are unable to log in, and existing sessions will be disconnected.

References

For more details and information about load balancer topologies, please read the documentation from your load balancer vendor for best practices.

Examples can be found in the VMware documentation at `https://pubs.vmware.com/horizon-62-view/index.jsp#com.vmware.horizon-view.planning.doc/GUID-955BC8CA-B662-43ED-BE39-50C96DF5B282.html`.

In addition to the VMware documentation, various resources exist to help plan and configure VMware Horizon View environments with load balancers: `http://vmfocus.com/2014/01/14/load-balancing-horizon-view-design/`.

LoadBalancer.org hosts a useful reference document regarding configuring VMware Horizon View with hardware load balancers and various technology configurations. Note that this is specifically written with LoadBalancer.org load balancers in mind, but it can be extended to other load balancers: `http://pdfs.loadbalancer.org/Vmware_View_Deployment_Guide.pdf`.

Summary

In this chapter, we covered various ways to implement load balancing and HA for a VMware Horizon View environment. We discussed the advantages and disadvantages of each method of DNS load balancers, Windows load balancers, and software/hardware load balancers. We examined the port VMware Horizon View uses for load balancing. We also examined the scenarios of failure and how the environment will behave for each incident.

In the next chapter, we will cover HA planning for floating and dedicated pools. We will discuss the basics of how to plan for host failures and maintain the VMs in each pool type.

4
HA Planning for Floating and Dedicated Pools

In this chapter, we will review strategies for providing High Availability for various types of VMware Horizon View desktop pools. We will discuss the different use cases for VMware View and the typical deployment scenarios regarding the different use cases. We will cover best practices and various considerations for each.

In this chapter, we will cover the following topics:

- Overview of pools
- Dedicated pools
- HA considerations for dedicated pools
- Floating pools
- HA considerations for floating pools
- Manual pools
- HA considerations for manual pools
- Remote desktop services pools
- Remote desktop services pool HA considerations

An overview of pools

VMware Horizon View provides administrators with the ability to automatically provision and manage pools of desktops. As part of the provisioning of desktops, we must consider how we will continue service for the individual users in the event of a host or storage failure. Generally, High Availability requirements fall into two categories for each pool. We can have stateless desktops, where the user information is not stored on the VM between sessions, and stateful desktops, where the user information is stored on the desktop between sessions.

Stateless desktops

In a stateless configuration, we are not required to store data on the virtual desktops between user sessions. This allows us to use local storage instead of shared storage for our HA strategies, as we can tolerate host failures without the use of shared disk.

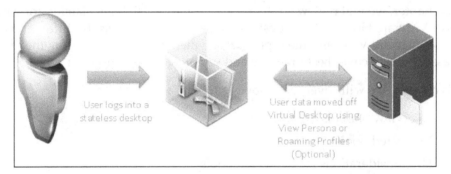

We can achieve a stateless desktop configuration using roaming profiles and/or View Persona profiles. This can greatly reduce cost and maintenance requirements for View deployments.

Stateless desktops are typical in the following environments:

- **Task workers**: A group of workers where the tasks are well known and they all share a common set of core applications. Task workers can use roaming profiles to maintain data between user sessions. In a multishift environment, having stateless desktops means we only need to provision as many desktops that will be used consecutively.

   Task worker setups are typically found in the following scenarios:

   ◦ Data entry
   ◦ Call centers

- ○ Finance, accounts payables, and accounts receivables
- ○ Classrooms (in some situations)
- ○ Laboratories
- ○ Healthcare terminals

- **Kiosk users**: A group of users that do not log in. Logins are typically automatic or without credentials. Kiosk users are typically untrusted users. Kiosk VMs should be locked down and restricted to only the core applications that need to be run. Kiosks are typically refreshed after logoff or at scheduled times after hours.

Kiosks can be found in situations such as the following:

- ○ Airline check-in stations
- ○ Library terminals
- ○ Classrooms (in some situations)
- ○ Customer service terminals
- ○ Customer self-service
- ○ Digital signage

Stateful desktops

Stateful desktops are desktops that require user data to be stored on the VM or the desktop host between user sessions.

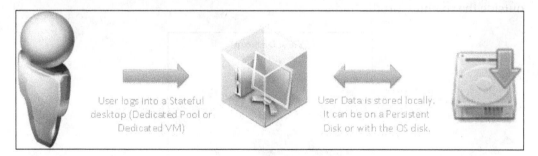

These machines are typically required by users who will extensively customize their desktop in complicated ways, require complex or unique applications that are not shared by a large group, or require the ability to modify their VM.

Stateful desktops are typically used for the following situations:

- Users who require the ability to modify the installed applications
- Developers
- IT administrators
- Unique or specialized users
- Department managers
- VIP staff/managers

Dedicated pools

Dedicated pools are View desktops provisioned using thin or thick provisioning. Dedicated pools are typically used for Stateful Desktop deployments. Each desktop can be provisioned with a dedicated persistent disk used for storing the user Profile and data. Once assigned, a desktop that user will always log into the same desktop ensuring that their profile is kept constant.

During OS refresh, balances, or recomposes, the OS disk is reverted back to the base image.

Dedicated pools with persistent disks offer simplicity for managing desktops as minimal profile management takes place. It is all managed by the View composer/ View connection server. It also ensures that applications that store profile data will almost always be able to retrieve the profile data on the next login. This means that the administrator doesn't need to track down applications that incorrectly store data outside the roaming profile folder.

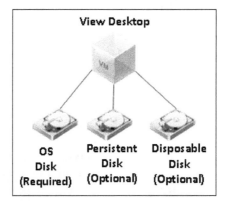

HA considerations for dedicated pools

Dedicated pools have very difficult HA requirements. Storing the user profile with the VM means that the VM has to be stored and maintained in a HA-aware fashion. This almost always results in a shared disk solution being required for dedicated pools. In the event of a host outage, other hosts connected to the same storage can start up the VM.

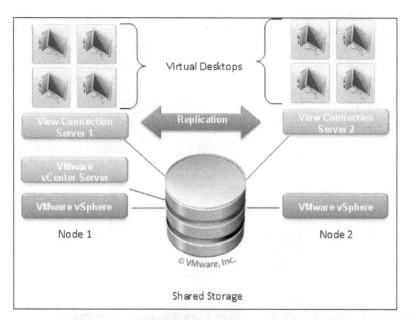

For shared storage, we can use NFS, ISCSI, Fiber channel, or VMware vSAN storage. Consider investing in storage systems with primary and backup controllers, as we will be dependent on the disk controllers being always available. Backups are also a must with this system as there are very few recovery options in the event of a storage array failure.

Floating pools

Floating pools are a pool of desktops where any user can be assigned to any desktop in the pool upon login. Floating pools are generally used for stateless desktop deployments. Floating pools can be used with roaming profiles or View persona to provide a consistent user experience on login. Since floating pools are treated as disposable VMs, we open up additional options for HA. Floating pools are given two local disks, the OS disk which is a replica from the assigned base VM, and the disposable disk where the page file, hibernation file, and temp drive are located. Depending on the View configuration, the OS disk can be refreshed on every logoff to ensure a consistent user experience. When floating pools are refreshed, recomposed, or rebalanced, all changes made to the desktop by the users are lost.

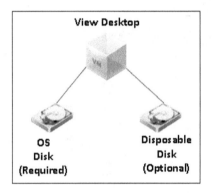

HA considerations for floating pools

Floating pools can be protected in several ways, depending on the environment.

Since floating pools can be deployed on local storage, we can protect against a host failure by provisioning the floating pool VMs on multiple separate hosts. In the event of a host failure, the remaining virtual desktops will be used to log users in. If there is free capacity in the cluster, more virtual desktops will be provisioned on other hosts.

For environments with shared storage, floating pools can still be deployed on the shared storage. But it is a good idea to have a secondary shared storage device or a highly available storage device. In the event of a storage failure, the VMs can be started on the secondary storage device. VMware Virtual SAN is inherently HA safe and there is no need for a secondary datastore when using Virtual SAN.

Many floating pool environments will utilize a profile management solution such as roaming profiles or View persona profiles. In these situations, it is essential to set up a redundant storage location for View profiles and/or roaming profiles. In practice, a Windows DFS share is a convenient and easy way to guard profiles against loss in the event of an outage. DFS can be configured to replicate changes made to the profile in real time between hosts. If the Windows DFS server is provisioned as VMs on shared storage, make sure to create a DRS rule to separate the VMs onto different hosts.

 For more information regarding Windows DFS, you can visit https://technet.microsoft.com/en-us/library/jj127250.aspx.

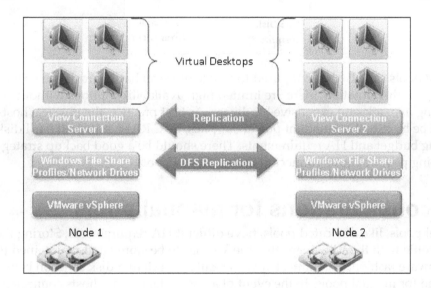

Manual pools

Manual pools are custom, dedicated desktops for each user. A VM is manually built for each user who is using the manual pool. Manual pools are stateful pools that generally do not utilize profile management technologies such as View persona or roaming profiles. Like dedicated pools, once a user is assigned to a VM, they will always log into the same VM. HA requirements for manual pools are very similar to dedicated pools. Manual desktops can be configured in almost any manner desired by the administrator. There are no requirements for more than one disk to be attached to the manual pool desktop.

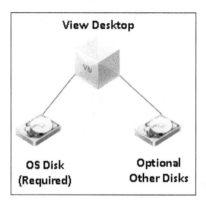

Manual pools can also be configured to utilize physical hardware as the virtual desktop. In this situation, there are limited high availability options without investing in exotic and expensive hardware. As best practice, the physical hosts should be built with redundant power supplies, ECC RAM, mirrored hard disks pending budget and HA requirements. There should be a good backup strategy for managing physical hosts connected to the manual pools.

HA considerations for manual pools

Manual pools, like dedicated pools, have difficult HA requirements. Storing the user profile with the VM means that the VM has to be stored and maintained in a HA-aware fashion. This almost always results in a shared disk solution being required for manual pools. In the event of a host outage, other hosts connected to the same storage can start up the VM.

For shared storage, we can use NFS, iSCSI, Fiber channel, or VMware vSAN storage. Consider investing in storage systems with primary and backup controllers, as we will be dependent on the disk controllers being always available. Backups are also a must with this system as there are very little recovery options in the event of a storage array failure. VSAN deployments are inherently HA-safe and are excellent candidates for manual pool storage.

Manual pools, given their static nature, also have the option to use replication technology to backup the VMs onto another disk. You can use VMware vSphere Replication and/or VMware SRM to do automatic replication or use a variety of storage replication solutions offered by storage and backup vendors.

In some cases, it may be possible to use fault tolerance on the virtual desktops for true high availability. Note that this would limit the individual VMs to a single vCPU, which may be undesirable.

Remote Desktop Services pools

Remote Desktop Services (RDS) pools are pools where the remote session or application is hosted on a Windows remote desktop server. The application or remote session is run under the users' credentials. Usually, all the user data is stored locally on the remote desktop server but can also be stored remotely using roaming profiles or View persona profiles. Typical uses of RDS are for migrating users off legacy RDS environments, hosting applications, and providing access to troublesome applications or applications with large memory footprints.

The Windows remote desktop server can be either a VM or a standalone physical host. It can be combined with Windows clustering technology to provide scalability and high availability. You can also deploy a load balancer solution to manage connections between multiple Windows remote desktop servers.

Remote desktop services pool HA considerations

Remote desktop services HA revolves around protecting individual RDS VMs or provisioning a cluster of RDS servers. When a single VM is deployed with RDS, it is generally best to use vSphere HA and clustering features to protect the VM. If the RDS resources are larger than practical for a VM, then we must focus on protecting individual host or clustering multiple hosts.

When the Windows remote desktop server is deployed as a VM, the following options are available:

- **Protect the VM with VMware HA using shared storage**: This allows vCenter to failover the VM to another host in the event of a host failure. vSphere will be responsible for starting the VM on another host. The VM will resume from a crashed state.

- **Protect the VM with VMware HA using VMware Virtual SAN**: This is same as the preceding point, but in this case the VM has been replicated to another host using Virtual SAN technology. The remote VM will be started up from a crashed state, using the last consistent hard drive image that was replicated.

- **Protect the VM using replication technologies such as vSphere Replication**: The VM will be periodically synchronized to a remote host. In the event of a host failure, we can manually activate the remotely synchronized VM.

- **Protect the VM using storage level replication**: In this case, we allow our storage vendor to provide replication technology to provide a redundant backup. This protects us in the event of a storage or host failure. These failures can be automated or manual. Consult with your storage vendor for more information.

- **Protect the VM using backup technologies**: This provides redundancy in the sense that we won't lose the VM if it fails. Unfortunately, you are at the mercy of your restore process to bring the VM back to life. The VM will resume from a crashed state. Always keep backups of production servers.

For RDS servers running on a dedicated server, we could utilize the following:

- **Redundant power supplies**: Redundant power supplies will keep the server going while a PSU is being replaced or becomes defective. It is also a good idea to have two separate power sources for each power supply. Simple things such as a power bar going faulty or tripping a breaker could bring down the server if there are not two independent power sources.

- **Uninterrupted power supply**: Battery backups are always a must for production-level equipments. Make sure to scale the UPS to provide adequate power and duration for your environment.

- **Redundant network interfaces**: In rare circumstances, a NIC can go bad or a cable can be damaged. In this case, redundant NICs will prevent a server outage. To protect against a switch outage, we should plug the NICs into separate switches.

- **Mirrored or redundant disks**: Hard drives are one of the most common failures in computers. Mirrored hard drives or RAID configurations are a must for production level equipment.

- **Two or more hosts**: Clustering physical servers will ensure that host failures won't cause downtime. Consider multisite configurations for even more redundancy.

Shared strategies for VMs and hardware:

- **Provide High Availability to the RDS using Microsoft Network Load Balancer (NLB)**: Microsoft NLB can provide load balancing to the RDS servers directly. In this situation, the clients would connect to a single IP managed by the NLB which would randomly be assigned to a server.

- **Provide High Availability using a load balancer to manage sessions between RDS servers**: A hardware or software load balancer can be used instead of Microsoft NLBs. Load balancer vendors provide a high variety of capabilities and features for their load balancers. Consult your load balancer vendor for best practices.

- **Use DNS round robin to alternate between RDS hosts**: This is one of the most cost-effective load balancing methods. It has the drawback of not being able to balance the load or to direct clients away from failed hosts. Updating DNS may delay adding new capacity to the cluster or delay removing a failed host from the cluster.

- **Remote desktop connection broker with High Availability**: We can provide RDS failover using the Connection Broker feature of our RDS server. For more details, visit. `https://technet.microsoft.com/en-us/library/ff686148%28WS.10%29.aspx`.

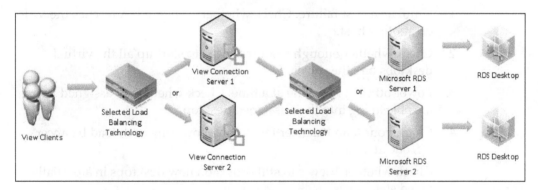

Here is an example topology using physical or virtual Microsoft RDS servers. We use a load balancing technology for the View connection servers as described in the previous chapter. We then will connect to the RDS via a load balancer, DNS round robin, or cluster IP.

High Availability checklist

Every HA cluster must be pushed to its limits in order to know where it will bend and where it will break. We want to test to ensure that any individual host or resource failure won't result in a total environment outage. To ensure your environment is ready for a failure, follow the tasks below and verify the environment is still functional:

- Steps for local storage-only clusters:

  1. Power off each host one at a time. Check whether all assigned users are able to log in to a desktop.

  2. Check your load balancer failover by powering each load balancer off, one at a time.

  3. Check whether enough resources exist to start up new virtual machines on other hosts.

  4. Check whether View can still provision new desktops.

  5. If using replication, check whether replicated VMs can be powered on for other hosts.

- Steps for shared storage clusters:

  1. Simulate a host failure. Check whether VMware HA rescues the VMs on another host.

  2. Check whether enough resources exist to start up all the virtual desktops on other hosts.

  3. Power off each host, one at a time. Check whether all assigned users are able to log into their assigned desktop.

  4. Check your load balancer failover by powering each load balancer off, one at a time.

  5. Check whether View can still provision new desktops in a partially failed state.

  6. Ensure redundant Windows DFS servers are setup with an anti-affinity DRS rule.

  7. Check all View anti-affinity rules as outlined in previous chapters.

  8. If using replication, check whether replicated VMs can be powered on in the other location.

- Steps for RDS clusters:

    1. Power off each RDS host/VM, one at a time. Check whether users can still get an RDS session or use an RDS application.

    2. Check your load balancer failover by powering each load balancer off, one at a time.

    3. If applicable, check whether the RDS farm/cluster is working and can serve clients on each RDS host.

    4. If applicable, check whether remote desktop connection broker High Availability is available.

Summary

In this chapter, we covered the concept of stateful and stateless desktops, as well as the consequences and techniques for supporting each in a highly available environment. We covered strategies for utilizing local storage only clusters and configuring shared storage environments.

In the next chapter, we will cover storage HA with VMware Virtual SAN. It can be used to provide highly available storage to clusters with local only storage. This is very useful for VMware View desktops and can be used to provide large amounts of compute resources without significant cost.

Storage HA with VMware Virtual SAN

In this chapter, we will go over the requirements and considerations for VMware Virtual SAN. We will cover disaster scenarios and configuration information to help with successful VMware Virtual SAN deployments.

We will cover the following topics:

- Virtual SAN capabilities and characteristics
- Virtual SAN for VMware Horizon View
- Virtual SAN sizing
- Virtual SAN installation
- Assigning a license to a Virtual SAN cluster
- Add a drive to a Virtual SAN
- Remove a drive from a Virtual SAN
- Virtual SAN features and best practices
- Virtual SAN HA best practices

Virtual SAN capabilities and characteristics

VMware Virtual SAN is a technology for combining the resources of multiple independent hosts connected only via a network connection into a single unified compute resource. VMware accomplishes this by replicating disk traffic with other hosts in the Virtual SAN cluster to provide High Availability with local storage. Virtual SAN can use hosts of multiple sizes and configurations in the same cluster.

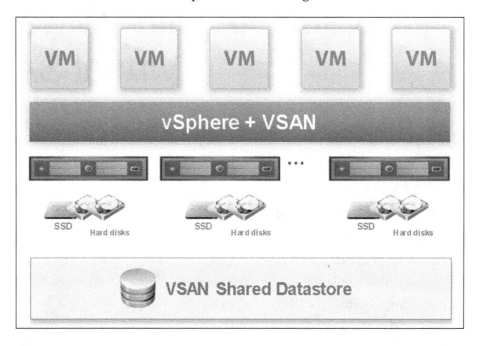

VMware Virtual SAN is designed to work directly with direct attached physical disks. Virtual SAN should be set up with direct disk access technologies on the local host. Virtual SAN will take care of all disk-related redundancies and storage computation on the host. Virtual SAN manages entire disks, including SSD and data disks; any disk added into Virtual SAN cannot have non-Virtual SAN data. Hardware RAID 0 is supported in Virtual SAN but carries a number of configuration requirements.

VMware Virtual SAN can be deployed using magnetic disks and flash disks. VMware Virtual SAN is capable of being used in what is called a Hybrid configuration. In this configuration, SSD storage and HDD storage are combined to produce a hybrid storage solution with characteristics of both drive types. Data that is frequently read or written is cached on the SSD storage. This provides fast read and write times. Inactive data is automatically moved to slower disks, active data is stored on the SSD to improve latency.

Virtual SAN separates the type of drive used into two categories:

- Cache layer: This is the SSD attached to each disk group
- Capacity layer: This is the hard drive or large capacity SSDs designed to store data long term

Virtual SAN is designed to recover from any individual disk failure. With the failure of a cache layer SSD the disk group is marked as degraded and disk IO and storage is moved to other disk groups. VMs won't notice the loss of a cache layer SSD. With the loss of a Capacity layer disk, the individual disk is marked as degraded and data is moved onto other drives. Virtual SAN automatically keeps redundant data on other disks in the cluster and/or disk groups.

Virtual SAN provides both performance and large storage savings to the storage administrator. Note that only the capacity disks contribute to the total storage available. For instance, a disk group with a 512 GB SSD and a 2 TB HDD will only have the storage capacity of 2 TB.

Virtual SAN can be deployed in what is called an **All Flash configuration**. In this configuration, fast reliable and durable SSDs are used for caching information and slower high capacity SSDs are used for long term storage. All Flash configurations require vSphere 6.0.

Virtual SAN can be utilized to provide a highly redundant storage environment that doesn't rely on shared storage technologies such as NFS, iSCSI or Fiber Channel. Virtual SAN can tolerate host failures without data loss. Virtual SAN is a hypervisor level technology; simply licensing Virtual SAN from VMware is enough to turn on a new Virtual SAN cluster. VMware Virtual SAN clusters can be grown on the fly by adding another host or adding additional storage or other resources to an existing host. Virtual SAN creates a single Virtual SAN datastore accessible to all hosts in the cluster, whether or not they have disks. Storage vMotion is supported with Virtual SAN. All hosts can also mount any other datastores, VMFS, or NFS.

Virtual SAN supports VMware features that require shared storage, such as HA, vMotion, and DRS.

Servers running on the Virtual SAN or other VMware datastores can be managed using storage polices. Virtual SAN uses these storage policies to dynamically protect and move VMs as resources and failures demand.

Virtual SAN can be managed using the existing vSphere Client or vSphere Web Client.

Virtual SAN introduces several unique constructs that impact the way in which view designs and sizing considerations are performed. The following are Virtual SAN constructs:

- **Disk groups**: These are composed of a cache layer and disk layer. Each disk group consists of one SSD and one or more capacity layer disks. In hybrid deployments the capacity layer has magnetic disks. In All Flash deployments the capacity layer has storage optimized flash.

- **Datastore**: Virtual SAN presents a datastore that can be used across multiple hosts. Virtual SAN datastores are protected from individual drive failures and host failures.

- **Objects**: Each file on the Virtual SAN is considered an object, and each object may be composed of components that may reside on multiple hosts or disks.

- **Components**: A component is a part of an object that is unique to each disk on each host. It can be thought of as a local file or data segment.

- **Network**: Virtual SAN utilizes the network extensively for disk traffic; at minimum, a dedicated 1 GB NIC is required.

- **Storage Policy Based Management** (**SPBM**): Virtual SAN utilizes storage policies to determine how it will manage each VM; storage polices determine the number of failures to tolerate and the stripe width of each VM.

Virtual SAN for VMware Horizon View

Combining Virtual SAN and VMware Horizon View offers several unique benefits to any environment. Virtual SAN uses local storage on your hosts that is often overlooked in favor of shared storage. It allows administrators to purchase hosts and grow the cluster on demand incrementally as our environment grows. We can build a cluster without costly SAN or NAS infrastructure. We can purchase hosts with only local storage. We get significant performance benefits from the hybrid flash architecture when used with VMware Horizon View. Reads from a link-cloned image are almost always cached on the SSD since multiple VMs will be requesting the same data frequently. In practice, we can get a read cache hit rate as high as 90%.

```
https://www.vmware.com/files/pdf/products/vsan/VMware-VSAN-5.5-
Evaluations-k.pdf
```

Pictured in the following illustration is a typical deployment of Virtual SAN with three hosts. We depict three disk groups (one for each host). Virtual SAN automatically stores the Virtual Desktops across the cluster in an $N + 1$ redundant fashion.

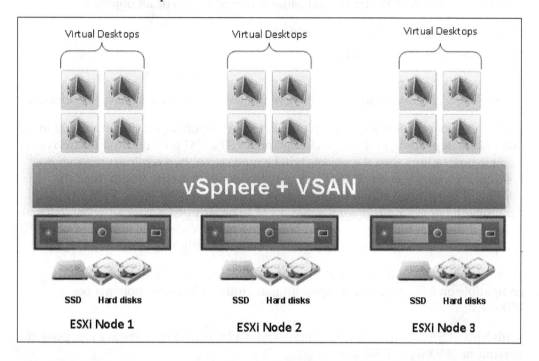

In addition to Virtual SAN caching, we have View Storage Accelerator. It is a fast in-memory, deduplicated read cache. View Storage Accelerator allocates memory residing on every host and uses the memory to store the most often read data. The in memory cache provides a near optimal cache layer for the virtual desktops.

For more information about Virtual SAN, please consult VMware documentation:

- `http://www.vmware.com/files/pdf/products/vsan/VSAN_Design_and_Sizing_Guide.pdf`
- `http://blogs.vmware.com/storage/files/2015/06/Horizon_View_6.0.2_VSAN_6.0_Hybrid_RA.pdf`

Components

Virtual machines are logically composed of a set of objects in Virtual SAN. Any VM item that create a new file on the datastore is considered to be an object:

- Each VMDK/VM disk is an object
- Each snapshot is an object
- Each VM swap space is an object
- Each VM home namespace (where the .vmx, log files, and so on are located)

Each object comprises a set of components. Each component may be replicated to other hosts depending on the VM storage policy. If a VM is configured to survive a single host failure, then the objects will be made up of two replica components residing on separate hosts. If the storage policy contains a strip width, then the object will be stripped across multiple devices in the capacity layer. Each strip is a component. For example, if we wanted a VM to be stripped across all seven disks in a disk group, then that VMDK object belonging to the VM would consist of seven components on seven different disks. The maximum strip width per object is 12.

With Virtual SAN on-disk format Version 1 (available on 5.5 and backwards compatible on 6.0), there is a component maximum of 3000 components per ESXi host.

With Virtual SAN on-disk format Version 2 (available on 6.0), there is a component maximum of 9000 per ESXi host.

The component size maximum is 255 GB; if a VMDK is created with a size that is larger than 255 GB, the VMDK object is automatically split into multiple components.

VMs can be configured to tolerate a maximum of three failures.

Virtual SAN cache mechanics

Whenever a VM or host requests data from a Virtual SAN datastore, the data is written into the read cache of the cache SSD. This sort of caching assumes that the data will likely be requested again in the near future for additional processing or may be requested by a different VM that reads the same data, such as link-cloned desktops. In addition to the section requested, the Virtual SAN will cache the entire 1 MB chunk in case it is read sequentially, such as during file reads, writes or copies.

Upon loading the data into the read cache, Virtual SAN will determine a segment of data to evict from the read cache. The evicted data is chosen based on how frequently it is read and the last time it was read. Infrequently read items are evicted from the read cache.

Virtual SAN replicates storage objects to multiple servers for protection purposes. Reads are distributed across the replicas of an object for better resource utilization. However, a certain range of logical addresses of an object is always read from the same replica. The benefits of this strategy are as follows:

- This strategy improves the chances that the object is in a read cache
- Data is not cached on more than one read cache

This design decision is designed to maximize the use of the flash cache, regardless of the location of the data. As a consequence of this, we should expect network traffic for both the read and write case of Virtual SAN. Most customers will use Virtual SAN with a 10 Gbps network. With 10 Gbps networking, the latency for a cached lookup on a remote host is less than the latency for reading from local magnetic disk. As such, this mechanic improves the clusters total performance as well as improving local read cache performance.

> For more information, please consult VMware documentation:
> `https://www.vmware.com/files/pdf/products/vsan/`
> `VMware-Virtual-SAN-Data-Locality.pdf`

Virtual SAN requirements and limitations

Virtual SAN has a particular set of limitations regarding storage, host, and network limitations. For best results, all the requirements of Virtual SAN should be met in a production environment.

Virtual SAN requirements for hybrid configurations:

- 1 GB NIC (dedicated) minimum, 10 GB NIC (shared) recommended.
- A VMkernel port configured on each network that VSAN traffic will be replicated.
- At least 6 GB of RAM per host, 10 GB when using seven or more disks.
- SATA/SAS HBA or RAID controller.
- At least 1 SSD in each host for hybrid configurations.
- Recommended that SSD storage is at least 10% of the total storage in capacity.
- A minimum of three hosts in a Virtual SAN cluster with storage disks; four is recommended.

- All Flash configurations with fast durable and slow and capacity require VSAN 6.0.

- Virtual SAN clusters can include hosts with storage disks, or without. The minimum requirement is three hosts with storage disks.

- Minimum version of vSphere: 5.5. Recommended version: 5.5 Update 2 or 6.0.

- Minimum version of vCenter: 5.5. Recommended version: 5.5 Update 2 or 6.0.

Virtual SAN requirements for All Flash configurations:

- 10 GB NIC is required.

- A VMkernel port configured on each network that VSAN traffic will be replicated.

- At least 6 GB of RAM per host, 10 GB when using seven or more disks.

- SSDs are used both as the cache layer and capacity layer.

- Capacity Layer SSDs must be marked as such.

- A minimum of three hosts in a Virtual SAN cluster with storage disks, recommended four.

- Virtual SAN clusters can include hosts with storage disks, or without. The minimum requirement is three hosts with storage disks.

- Minimum version of vSphere: 6.0.

- Minimum version of vCenter: 6.0.

Every Virtual SAN deployment should be deployed on hardware on the VMware Hardware Compatibility list. This will ensure both optimum performance from VMware software and VMware support will be able to quickly rule out any hardware compatibility issues.

 The hardware compatibility list can be found at: `http://vmware.com/go/virtualsan-hcl`

Virtual SAN limits and limitations:

- Up to 32 hosts in a Virtual SAN cluster in vSphere 5.5.

- Up to 64 hosts in a Virtual SAN cluster in vSphere 6.0.

- No more than 100 virtual machines per host in vSphere 5.5.

- No more than 200 virtual machines per host in vSphere 6.0.
- No more than 3200 virtual machines in a cluster in vSphere 5.5.
- No more than 6400 virtual machines in a cluster in vSphere 6.0.
- vSphere HA can protect up to 2048 virtual machines per Virtual SAN cluster in vSphere 5.5.
- vSphere HA can protect up to 6400 virtual machines per Virtual SAN Cluster in vSphere 6.0.
- A maximum of five disk groups per vSphere host.
- A maximum of seven magnetic disks per disk group in hybrid deployments.
- A maximum of one flash device for cache per disk group in hybrid deployments.
- A maximum of seven flash disks in the capacity layer in All Flash deployments.
- A maximum of one flash device for cache per disk group in All Flash deployments.
- 35 magnetic disks per host (five disk groups with seven drives) in hybrid deployments.
- 35 capacity flash disk per host (five disk groups with seven drives) in All Flash deployments.
- Five flash disks used for the cache layer (five disk groups with one cache drive).
- Virtual SAN 5.5 (on disk version 1) does not support VMDKs that are sized larger than 2 TB.
- Virtual SAN 6.0 (on disk version 2) does not support VMDKs that are sized larger than 62 TB.
- Virtual SAN supports only SATA, SAS HDD, and PCIe storage. It doesn't support NFS, USB, Fiber Channel, or iSCSI.
- Virtual SAN doesn't support fault tolerance, vSphere DPM, and Storage I/O control.
- Virtual SAN does not support SE Sparse disks.
- Virtual SAN does not support SCSI reservations.
- Virtual SAN does not support RDM, VMFS, diagnostic partition, and other disk access features.
- At least three hosts in a Virtual SAN cluster must contribute local storage.

- Hosts can only access the Virtual SAN storage if they are part of the cluster.
- Not all hosts need to contribute local storage to the Virtual SAN cluster.

> For creating a Virtual SAN Cluster with 64 hosts, see the VMware KB 2110081:
>
> ```
> http://kb.vmware.com/selfservice/microsites/
> search.do?language=en_US&cmd=displayKC&externa
> lId=2110081
> ```

Virtual SAN sizing

Virtual SAN has a number of unique requirements to consider when sizing a server. Servers hosting a Virtual SAN should have fast network speeds, ideally 10 Gbps or multiple 1 Gbps connections. Virtual SAN clusters require a minimum of three hosts with local storage to function. For best redundancy, four or more hosts are recommended as rebuilding of VM redundancy can occur automatically with four servers. Each server requires a minimum of one SSD disk and one spinning disk or two SSD disks. For large storage capacity, we would look for many 2.5" bays or 3.5" bays with hot swap capability.

CPU requirements

Processor requirements can be tricky to calculate, but generally we want to find a ratio of vCPU to CPU cores on the host. Based on real world tests, VMware has published the following recommendations regarding vCPU to CPU ratios:

- 1:1 to 3:1 no performance problems noted, VM run near optimally.
- 3:1 to 5:1 performance degradation noted on VMs.
- 6:1 high vCPU contention and VM performance suffers.
- In addition to the vCPU, we must consider the number of VMs per host.
- Virtual SAN 5.5 has a maximum of 100 VMs per host.
- Virtual SAN 6.0 has a maximum of 200 VMs per host.
- Virtual SAN usually adds approximately 15% CPU overhead over a regular VM. CPUs should be allocated to account for the increased CPU requirements of Virtual SAN.

SSD requirements

The SSD cache in Virtual SAN should be approximately 10% of the total storage capacity to maximize the cache performance.

Virtual SAN also requires certain endurance requirements from the SSDs used in the solution. Since SSD cache drives will be constantly read and written, we should use SSDs that meet the following endurance requirements.

Endurance requirements for SAS and SATA flash devices:

- The drive must support at least 10 **drive writes per day (DWPD)**
- The drive must support random write endurance up to 3.5 PB on 8 KB transfer size per NAND module or up to 2.5 PB on 4 KB transfer size per NAND module

Endurance requirements for PCIe flash devices:

- The drive must support at least 10 drive writes per day
- The drive must support random write endurance up to 3.5 PB on 8 KB transfer size per NAND module or up to 2.5 PB on 4 KB transfer size per NAND module

Hard drive requirements

We need a certain performance standard from our magnetic disk hard drives. Typically, these drives are found in 7200, 10,000, and 15,000 RPM. For most storage arrays 7200 or 10,000 will provide enough throughput, since our SSD cache will handle the majority of the fast IO. Note that SAS drives have a 15% performance boost over regular SATA drives when used with Virtual SAN. When possible, we should utilize SAS drives to maximize performance.

VMware requires that any magnetic HDD meet the following minimum endurance metrics:

- The drive must have a minimum useful life of 5 years
- The drive must meet an **annualized failure rate (AFR)** of no more than 0.73% or **mean time between failures (MTBF)** of 1,200,000 hours

Network requirements

Virtual SAN requires at least 1 Gbps NIC that is dedicated to Virtual SAN or a 10 Gbps NIC that is shared with other traffic. All Flash configurations require 10 Gbps networking.

A VMkernel adapter must be configured on each network being used for Virtual SAN replication. See the *Virtual SAN installation* section for more details.

Virtual SAN does not support multiple VMkernel adapters on the same subnet. Multiple VMkernel NICs do not offer load-balancing advantages. Multiple VMkernel adapters on different networks, such as VLAN or separate physical fabric, are supported.

All hosts participating in Virtual SAN should be on a single L2 network, which has multicast (IGMP snooping) enabled. If the hosts participating in Virtual SAN span across multiple switches or even across L3 boundaries, the network must allow multicast connectivity. You can change multicast addresses from the defaults if your network environment requires, or if you are running multiple Virtual SAN clusters on the same L2 network.

When Virtual SAN and vSphere HA are enabled for the same cluster, the VMware HA traffic goes over the storage network rather than the management network. The management network is used by vSphere HA only when Virtual SAN is disabled.

Blade servers

Blade servers usually are not ideal for Virtual SAN solutions. The limited number of local storage devices prevents meaningful capacity from being added to the cluster and the proprietary network equipment often means higher costs for network add-in cards and 10 Gbps networking. It is very rare that a blade will be able to have a PCIe SSD card installed due to the form factor. Blades can be utilized as compute only nodes in Virtual SAN environments, but then all IO will be handled by other hosts and will always utilize the network stack for read and writes to disk. This can congest both the host that the VM is stored on and the blade server the VM is running on. Finally, Virtual SAN doesn't support external storage enclosures, which restricts storage options for blade servers.

Rack servers

Rack servers provide the ideal platform for Virtual SAN, providing both redundant hardware and a large amount of expandability. Rack servers tend to be deployed in 1U configurations where more CPU is required than storage. When more storage is required, 2U, 3U, or 4U servers are more common since there is often a significant increase in available 3.5" or 2.5" hard drive bays. Rack servers also have plenty of PCIe slots to allow a fast low latency PCIe SSD to be installed, further improving performance.

 For more information regarding Virtual SAN sizing, please see the Virtual SAN sizing tool on VMware's website:

`https://vsantco.vmware.com/vsan/SI/SIEV`

Virtual SAN installation

Virtual SAN installation is fairly straight forward. We simply need to license Virtual SAN on three ESXi hosts and configure them for Virtual SAN.

1. Install ESXi on at least three hosts and configure them to suit the environment. At least three hosts must contribute storage to the Virtual SAN cluster.

2. Set up and install a vCenter Server or vCenter appliance to manage the 3+ ESXi hosts.

3. Set up the networking for Virtual SAN. Hosts with 1 Gbps networking require one or more dedicated NICs and will require their own vSwitch or Distributed vSwitch. All the hosts should have their Virtual SAN vSwitch named the same. Hosts with 10 Gbps can use a shared network for Virtual SAN traffic. It is recommended that you segregate Virtual SAN traffic from all other traffic.

4. Configure a VMkernel port on the vSwitch for use with Virtual SAN. This requires that the VMkernel port be configured for Virtual SAN traffic.

    1. In the vSphere Web Client, navigate to the host.

    2. Select the **Manage** tab and click on **Networking**.

3. Select **VMkernel adapters** and click on **Add host networking**.

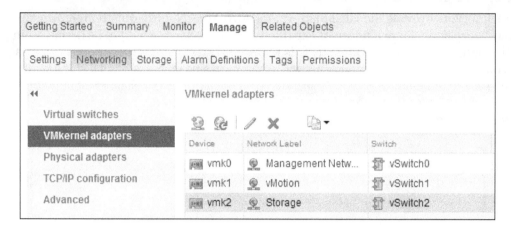

4. On the **Select connection** type page, select **VMkernel Network Adapter** and click on **Next**.

5. Configure a target device.

6. On the **Port properties** page, select Virtual SAN traffic.

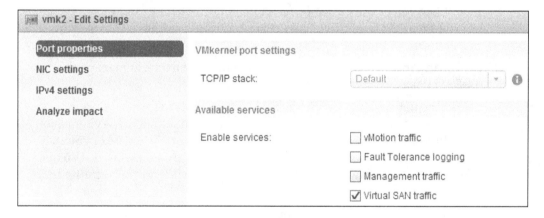

7. Complete the VMkernel adapter configuration.

8. Verify that the Virtual SAN column shows enabled as the status for the VMkernel adapter.

5. If the hosts are not already part of a cluster, create a cluster and add the hosts to the new cluster. Optionally, steps 6–11 can be done while creating the cluster.

6. Log into the vSphere Web Client.

7. Navigate to the cluster where we will enable Virtual SAN.

8. Navigate to **Manage** | **Settings**.

9. Under the **Virtual SAN** column on the left side, select **General**.

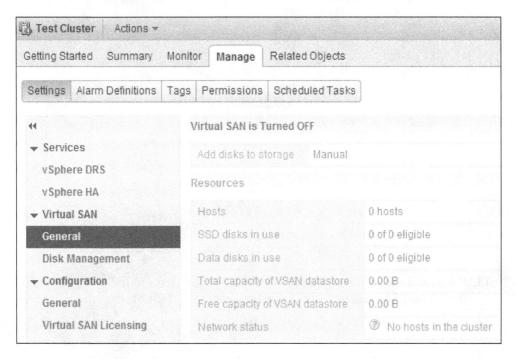

10. Right of **Virtual SAN is Turned OFF,** hit **Edit....**

11. Select the checkbox **Turn ON Virtual SAN**. You may be required to temporarily disable vSphere HA if it is enabled on the cluster.

12. Under **Add disks to storage**, select one of the following settings:
    - **Manual**: Select each disk that will be a part of the Virtual SAN will be manually added and configured.
    - **Automatic**: Virtual SAN will select all eligible disks for you and add them.

These settings are shown in the following screenshot:

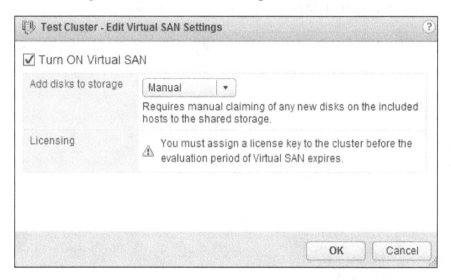

13. If **Manual** mode was selected, we will now add disks to the disk groups. In the Virtual SAN section of the cluster, select the **Disk Management** section.

14. Select the **Claim Disks** button and select the drives for the Virtual SAN to manage.

15. Create a disk group and select the SSD and storage drives for use with the Virtual SAN.

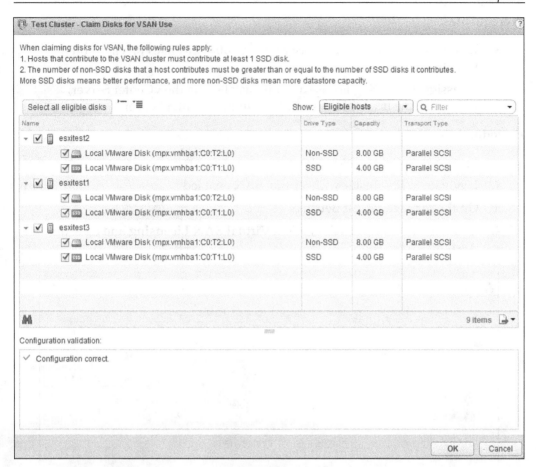

16. You should now have a VSAN datastore that you can utilize as shared storage when creating VMs.

Assign a license key to the Virtual SAN cluster

When Virtual SAN is enabled on a cluster for the first time, the user is given an automatic 60-day trial. If you want to continue using Virtual SAN, the cluster must be licensed with Virtual SAN.

Prerequisites:

- Requires the administrative user have **Global.Licenses** privilege on the vCenter Server.

- To assign an existing license already installed on the vCenter Server, verify that the license key is available in the vCenter Server.

Procedure:

1. Launch the vSphere Web Client.

2. Navigate to the cluster with Virtual SAN enabled.

3. On the **Manage** tab hit **Settings**.

4. In the configuration section, select **Virtual SAN Licensing** and click on **Assign License Key...**.

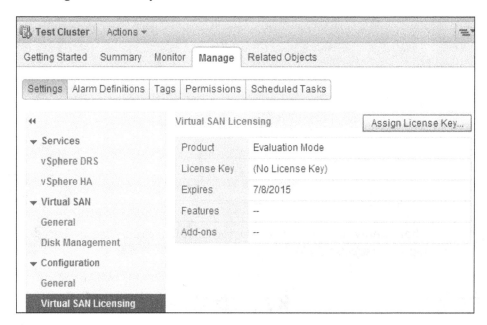

5. Select one of the following licensing options:

    1. Assign an existing license key. Select an existing license key from the license inventory. Click on **OK**.

    2. Assign a new license key. Enter the license key and optional label. Click on **Decode,** then click on **OK**.

Add a drive into a Virtual SAN

Here we will examine how to add a drive to the Virtual SAN. Drives included in a Virtual SAN can be added to a disk group.

1. Log into the vSphere Web Client.

2. Navigate to the Virtual SAN cluster.

3. Navigate to the **Manage** tab, then select **Settings**.

4. Under **Virtual SAN,** select **Disk Management**.

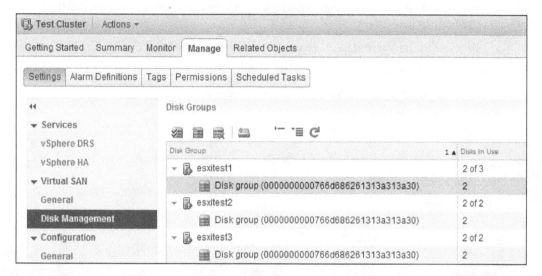

5. Select the disk group to add the disk to. Click the **Add a disk to the selected disk group** icon 🛢.

6. Select the disk to add and click on **OK**.

7. The disk should appear on the list of disks that belong to the disk group.

Remove a drive from a Virtual SAN

Here we will examine how to remove a drive from the Virtual SAN. Drives removed from the Virtual SAN will be removed from their associated disk groups.

1. Log into the vSphere Web Client.

2. Navigate to the host with a drive to replace.

3. Place the host into maintenance mode.

4. When placing a Virtual SAN host into maintenance mode, you will be prompted to select an evacuation mode. Generally, **Ensure accessibility** is the best to use.

5. Browse to the Virtual SAN cluster in the vSphere Web Client navigator.

6. Click on the **Manage** tab and click on **Settings**.

7. Under **Virtual SAN**, click on **Disk Management**.

8. Select the host to modify.

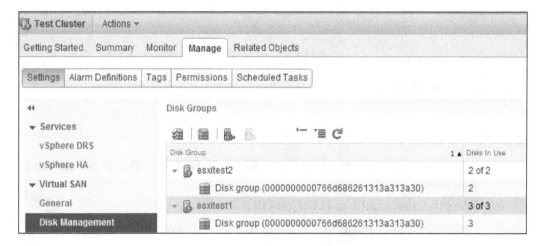

9. Remove a disk group or selected disks.

   1. To remove a disk group, select the **Remove the Disk Group** option. Select the disk group to remove and click on the **Remove Disk Group** icon.

   2. To remove a disk, select the **Remove the Selected Disk** option. Under **Disk Groups,** select the disk group with the failed disk. Under **Disks,** select the disk to be removed.

10. Navigate back to the affected host.

11. Select **Exit Maintenance Mode** for the affected host.

Virtual SAN features and best practices

Here we will examine the various features and best practices that encompass Virtual SAN. We will examine multiple failure scenarios and ways to plan around them.

Virtual SAN hardware best practices

When provisioning Virtual SAN hosts, it is important to consider the various failure scenarios that can happen. The most common failure, being hard drive failure, requires the data on the drive to be moved to another device. This happens automatically in the case of a hardware fault. Or can be manually triggered by deleting the disk from the vCenter GUI. Virtual SAN clusters should always have enough resources to tolerate a single host failure. Close monitoring will be required to ensure the resources don't expand past the single host failure scenario. If the hosts are not identical, then we must have enough free resources to match the largest host or host with the largest capacity of each resource.

Given that multiple host failures are problematic for Virtual SAN, we should ensure that our hosts are using resources such that no resource failure causes a loss of quorum. For example, if two of our three hosts are using the same power source (say power bar or circuit) and the breaker flips, our cluster will lose quorum since two of three hosts are not in the cluster any more. The other consideration is networking. At minimum we want the hosts fully connected to two switches for switch redundancy. This would allow the cluster to survive a switch or link failure.

Virtual SAN maintenance mode

Before performing maintenance tasks such as host upgrades, hardware replacement, or decommissioning we should place the Virtual SAN host into maintenance mode. In maintenance mode, the host is temporarily removed from cluster duty.

We have a number of options available to us to determine maintenance mode behavior when it comes to Virtual SAN.

Option	Description
Ensure accessibility	In this mode, VMs with replicas on other host are simply migrated to other hosts using vMotion. VMs that are not configured with a replica will have the replica moved to other hosts to ensure they are still accessible during this host's maintenance mode.

Option	Description
Full data evacuation	Virtual SAN evacuates all data to other hosts in the cluster. This option results in the largest amount of data transfer and consumes the most time and resources. This option is only necessary if you plan to remove the host permanently.

The host will not enter maintenance mode if a virtual machine object that has data on the host is not accessible and cannot be fully evacuated. |
| No data evacuation | No data is removed from the host. If the host is powered off or removed, the VMs with data only on the host will become inaccessible. |

Virtual SAN storage policy management

Virtual SAN follows a set of storage policies when determining the storage and performance requirements of each VM. We can use Virtual SAN storage policies to manage where and how the VMs are stored on the Virtual SAN datastore. Virtual SAN uses the VASA interface with vCenter to communicate a set of the datastore capabilities to vCenter Server. Using vCenter we can specify what VMs are stored where and how they should be stored.

For VMware Horizon View, we generally want to set the number of failures to tolerate to 0 for floating pools and to 1 or more for dedicated pools.

Virtual SAN storage policies have the following attributes:

Capability	Description
Number of failures to tolerate	The number of host failures this VM should tolerate. For n failures tolerated, n + 1 copies are created. Default value 1, maximum value 3.
Number of disk stripes per object	The number of HDD across which the replica of the virtual machine is striped. A value higher than 1 may increase performance but uses more system resources. The default value is 1, maximum value 12.
Object space reservation	The percentage of the logical size of the object that should be reserved or thick provisioned during virtual machine creation. The rest of the object is thin provisioned. Thick provisioned VMs have 100% of their capacity reserved automatically.

Default value is 0%. Maximum value is 100%. |

Capability	Description
Flash read cache reservation	The percentage of the logical size of the VM that should be allocated and reserved for in the read cache. This setting should only be used if encountering read performance issues. This setting will reserve read cache such that other VMs are unable to use the read cache allocated. The remaining read cache is fairly divided by the remaining VMs. The default value is 0 percent while the maximum value is 100 percent.
	Note that by default Virtual SAN allocates read cache based on demand and is considered the most flexible and optimal configuration.
	Note that increasing this reservation may starve other VMs of read cache, resulting in a total loss of performance. Over provisioned read caches will result in a net loss of performance.
Force provisioning	If this is set to "yes", the object will be provisioned even if the data store cannot satisfy the constraints placed on the object by the storage policy.
	Use this parameter in bootstrapping scenarios and during an outage when standard provisioning is no longer possible.
	If this is set to "no" is used for the vast majority of Virtual SAN environments. Virtual SAN attempts to provision a virtual machine even when all requirements cannot be met.

To set up a storage policy, we can do the following:

1. Log into the vSphere Web Client.
2. Navigate to **Rules and Profiles | VM Storage Policies**.
3. Click on the **Create a New VM Storage Policy** icon.

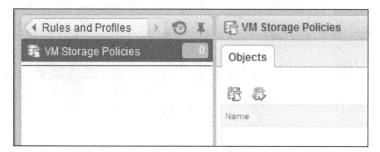

4. Select the vCenter instance to create the policy under.

5. Enter a name and description for the new storage policy.

6. Define the first rule set on the **Rule-Set 1** screen.

    1. Select VSAN from the **Rules based on vendor specific capabilities** dropbox.

    2. Add a capability and specify its value. Enter a value that is in the range of values provided by the capability profile of the Virtual SAN datastore.

    3. You can optionally add the tag based capabilities.

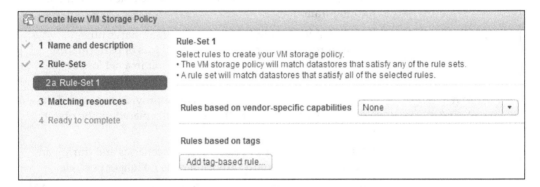

7. View the list of datastores that match this policy. Datastores must satisfy at least one rule set and all the individual rules within the rule set. Ensure the datastores you were expecting match the rule set.

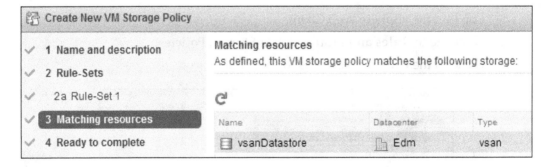

8. Click on **Finish**.

Storage policies for VMware Horizon View

For VMware Horizon View we will want to assign a storage policy to the View Connection Servers, vCenter Servers, View Composer Server, Active Directory Servers, View Security Servers, and Dedicated Pool Desktops. At minimum we want to assign a Number of Failures to Tolerate to 1.

Multiple host failures and quorum

After multiple host failures, there are cases where quorum may be lost. In the case of lost quorum, we will need to restore the host with the latest copy of the VM first. vSphere HA is unable to power on VMs if the host with the latest copy is not available.

For example, assume we have three hosts, H1, H2, H3. Assume that H1 fails followed by H2. Now all the cluster resources will have migrated on to H3. Assuming H3 fails then H2 and or H1 have been brought back online. H2 will have a full but dated copy of H3's VMs but will be unable to power them on due to the VM being out of date. Only upon H3's restoration will the Virtual SAN cluster be able to power on the VMs.

Admission control

One of the common pitfalls when configuring a highly available environment is the mismatch of the vSphere HA cluster admission control policy with the Virtual SAN **Number of failures to tolerate** setting. Importantly the vSphere HA admission control setting must be set to tolerate a lower number of host failures than the **Number of failures to tolerate** setting in Virtual SAN.

For example, if the Virtual SAN **Number of failures to tolerate** setting is set to two hosts, then vSphere HA Admission Control must be set to two or less hosts failed.

High Availability checklist

In order to verify that your environment is highly available, check the following failure scenarios to ensure that the environment can handle them:

- Power off each host and verify all the VMs are migrated and powered on, on other hosts
- Verify there are enough resources for a single host failure
- Power off the switch and verify the backup switch is configured correctly
- Test single NIC failure for each host

Summary

In this chapter, we covered the topics of Virtual SAN and how we can utilize it for our VMware Horizon View Desktops. We learned how to deploy and manage the Virtual SAN. We learnt the characteristics of the Virtual SAN and how it operates. We also covered how to handle failure cases of the Virtual SAN and general recovery steps.

In the next chapter, we will cover Fiber Channel storage where we will learn about Fiber Channel and how to deploy Fiber Channel SAN networks in a highly available fashion.

6
Hardware Redundancy Planning for Fibre Channel Storage

Fibre Channel architecture is inherently designed to provide low latency, highly reliable connections between servers and storage arrays. We will explore the basics of Fibre Channel high availability, and how to optimize and scale Fibre Channel to suite your environment.

In this chapter we will cover:

- Fibre Channel concepts and definitions
- How Fibre Channel works as a protocol
- Single controller Fibre Channel storage arrays
- Dual controller Fibre Channel storage arrays
- Planning for high availability
- How to manage Fibre Channel from within VMware
- High availability checklist

Fibre Channel concepts and definitions

A Fibre Channel is a channel based networking protocol designed to provide high throughput, high reliability, and low latency. To achieve this, the **Fibre Channel Protocol (FCP)** was designed to interface over high speed links (usually fiber optics but copper versions are also available). Fibre Channel is available in 2 Gbps, 4 Gbps, 8 Gbps, and 16 Gbps connections.

A Fibre Channel like Ethernet is only a base for other protocols. It can be used for IP, SCSI, and several other protocols. Typically, it is found running SCSI commands between servers and disk controllers or on SAN networks.

The following concepts are found in Fibre Channel jargon:

- **Host Bus Adapter (HBA)**: A physical interface for the server to communicate with other Fibre Channel devices.

- **Storage Processor (SP)**: The storage process or storage controller processes storage commands from other Fibre Channel devices. It's typically found on storage arrays.

- **Storage Area Network (SAN)**: A network composed of Fibre Channel hosts, switches, SPs, HBAs, and all storage devices that can communicate on the local Fibre Channel network. This is similar to a LAN in Ethernet networking.

- **Small Computer System Interface (SCSI)**: The standard communication protocol used for communicating between physical disks, hosts, storage controllers, and peripherals such as CD drives or scanners. SCSI is one of the most common protocols found running over Fibre Channel.

- **Logical Unit Number (LUN)**: A LUN is a logical unit number of a device addressed by the SCSI protocol. It will uniquely identify the storage volume on a SAN network.

- **Path/multipath**: A path a unique path through the SAN topology from the host to the storage processor. Multipathing refers to SAN topologies where multiple paths exist from the host to the storage processor. In highly available environments, we will always prefer a multipath setup to a single path setup.

- **Virtual Machine File System (VMFS)**: VMFS is the underlying file system for VMware ESXi on SAN storage. It permits the storage of VMs and VM snapshots to be accessed from multiple hosts. Multiple servers can read and write to the same file system.

Fibre Channel supports three topologies:

- **Point-to-Point (FC-P2P)**: In this topology, Fibre Channel is used to directly connect two devices, such as a server and storage array. This is the simplest Fibre Channel connection possible. All messages are targeted and processed by the other member of the Fibre Channel network. We can utilize multiple Fibre Channel links in the same P2P network to ensure redundancy in case of a link failure. Fibre Channel can automatically find a separate failover route in the event of a failure, since the disk controller will appear on both links. The maximum number of ports in a P2P connection is 2. The following diagram shows a FC-P2P network:

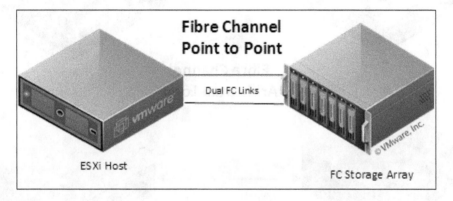

- **Arbitrated Loop (FC-AL):** An Arbitrated Loop Fibre Channel network resembles an Ethernet token network. In such a network, all the devices are connected together in a large loop. If a device is added to the network or a device fails the loop is broken, and the topology is rebuilt by the FCP. Generally, an Arbitrated Loop is rarely used in practice due to the failure potential and the inability to add or remove capacity on the fly. The maximum number of ports on a FC-AL is 127. All links in the Fibre Channel loop must be the same speed. The following diagram shows a FC-AL network:

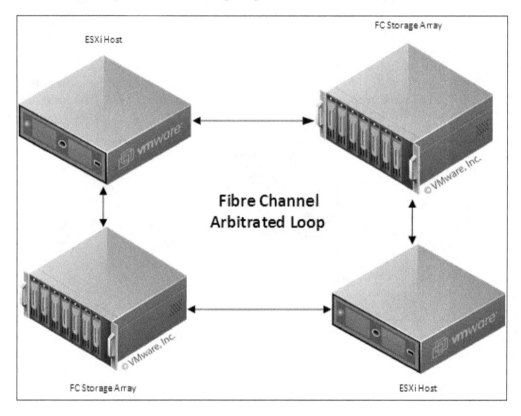

- **Switched Fabric (FC-SW):** All devices are connected together via a Fibre Channel switch. This topology is very similar to Ethernet switching except Fibre Channel is not susceptible to topology looping issues. The Fibre Channel switch will manage the link state of the Fibre Channel. It will only route traffic to the hosts addressed by the FCP. Failure of a single port is isolated and will not affect the other Fibre Channel hosts. Redundant pairs can be used to carry Fibre Channel traffic simultaneously. Fibre Channel switching allows for a mix of FC ports and speeds. Fibre Channel Switches can support up to 224 ports on the network. The following diagram shows a FC-SW network:

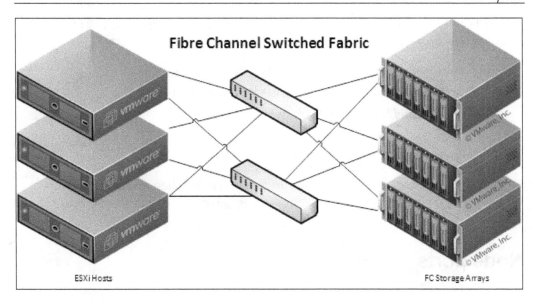

Fibre Channel layers

Fibre Channel is logically separated into five protocol layers.

We will now discuss each protocol layer:

- **Protocol Mapping Layer (FC4)**: This is where top level protocols perform their functions. Here we find SCSI and IP protocols on the Fibre Channel stack.

- **Common Services Layer (FC3)**: This is a thin layer that could eventually implement functions such as encryption or RAID redundancy algorithms and multiport connections.

- **Network Layer (FC2)**: This is defined by the FC-PI-2 standard. It defines the main protocols and port-to-port connections. This is where network topology and connection state logic come into play and define the bulk of the FCP.

- **Data Link Layer (FC1)**: Here we find the logic for line coding of signals and data transport.

- **Physical Layer (FC0)**: This includes cabling, connectors etc.

Layers FC0 through FC2 are also known as **FC-PH**, the physical layers of Fibre Channel. The Fibre Channel components operates in following layers:

- Fibre Channel switches operate in the FC0 to FC2 range
- Fibre Channel routers operate in the FC0 to FC4 range
- Fibre Channel hubs operate on the FC0 layer

Fibre Channel ports

Fibre Channel is defined and organized into port types. When a SAN network is being created, it is useful to keep in mind each type of port available and how they are used.

Node ports

There are various node ports that can be described as follows:

- **N_port**: N_port is a port on the node (a host or storage device) and is used with both FC-P2P and FC-SW topologies. This is the most common port found in Fibre Channel topologies.
- **NL_port**: NL_port is a Node Loop Port and is exclusively found in FC-AL topology. Traffic to the NL_port will be repeated onto the next hop if not addressed locally.
- **F_port**: F_port is a port on the switch that connects to an N_port. It's also known as fabric port. No looping occurs on an F_port.
- **FL_port**: FL_port is a port on the switch that connects to a FC-AL loop (other NL_ports). It is called a fabric loop port.
- **E_port**: E_port is used to connect two Fibre Channel Switches together. It is called an Expansion port. E_port links two switches to form an inter-switch link (ISL).
- **B_port**: A bridge port is a Fabric inter-element port used to connect bridge devices with E_Ports on a switch. The B_port provides a subset of the E_port functionality. B_ports are commonly found on port converters and adapters.
- **D_port**: D_port is a diagnostic port. It is used for the purpose of doing link-level diagnostics between switches and to track down link level faults on a port.
- **EX_port**: EX_port is a connection between a Fibre Channel router and a Fibre Channel switch. On a switch it is labeled as an E_port. On the router it is labeled as an EX_port.

- **TE_port**: TE_port is an extended ISL or EISL. The TE_port provides standard E_port functions and routing of multiple **Virtual SANs (VSANs)**. The Fibre Channel frame is modified upon ingress/egress of the VSAN environment (VSAN tagging). Sometimes referred to as a Trunking E_port.

- **Auto or auto-sensing port**: It can automatically become an E_, TE_, F_, or FL_port as needed.

The following is a diagram of the various ports and switch interconnects. Knowledge of each port type will be required when configuring FC storage networks:

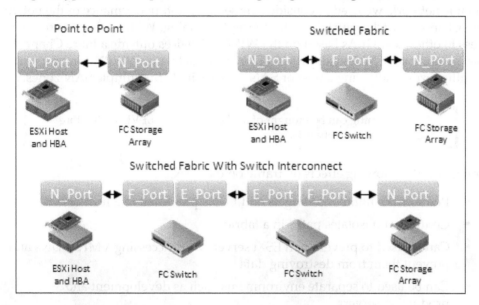

Fibre Channel port attributes

When Fibre Channel ports are connected to a SAN network, we have several attributes that can be used to address and identify the ports. Ports can be identified in the following ways:

- **World Wide Port Name (WWPN)**: This is a globally unique identifier for the FC port, similar in properties to the MAC address in Ethernet networking. The FC switches will discover the WWPN and assign a port address to the device.

- **Port_ID (or port address)**: Whenever an FC port is plugged into an FC switch, the port is assigned a Port_ID (similar to an IP address in TCP/IP networking). This unique ID enables routing of data through the SAN network to the individual ports. The Port_ID is only valid while the device is logged into the switch.

The preceding attributes allow us to utilize **N_port ID Virtualization** (**NPIV**). In this way, a single FC HBA port (N_port) can register with several WWPNs. This allows the HBA/FC port to claim multiple fabric addresses, each unique to the SAN. The ESXi host can utilize NPIV to give a VM an individual virtualized FC port. This allows a VM to be assigned its own LUN on a SAN.

Fibre Channel zoning

Since Fibre Channel is a networked protocol with multiple hosts having access to the same network, we need to consider the security and performance of the network. Fibre Channel switches introduce the concept of zoning. With zoning, we restrict access to other host HBAs based on the WWPN. Devices outside a Fibre Channel zone are not visible to devices inside a Fibre Channel zone. WWPN can be a part of multiple zones allowing a host or SAN to participate in multiple SAN zones.

 Zoning can be thought of as the equivalent of VLAN in Fibre Channel networks.

Zoning has the following effects on traffic on the SAN:

- Reduces the number of targets and LUNs presented to a host or VM
- Controls and isolates paths in a fabric
- Can be used to prevent non ESXi servers from accessing VMFS LUNs and prevent them from destroying data
- Can be used to separate environments such as development and production servers
- Zoning can reduce the effect of misconfiguration issues

Zoning normally comes in two varieties:

- **Single initiator zoning**: In this zoning situation, the zone is based on a single host with storage arrays added to the zone. The host is prevented from talking to other hosts on the network and also from talking to storage arrays that it doesn't have access too. This is the preferred zoning method for VMware ESXi hosts.
- **Target initiator zoning**: The zone is set up based on the storage array. The hosts added to the zone the storage array belongs to. This setup has the downside of letting the hosts communicate with each other, which may be undesirable from a security perspective since the SAN is usually more trusted.

VMFS and Fibre Channel workflow

It is a shared file system that multiple ESXi hosts can read and write to, simultaneously. VMFS is used to store all aspects of the VM including but not limited to: VMDK disks, snapshots, configuration data and swap data.

When a VM wants to read or write to a disk located on the SAN, the following must take place:

1. The guest operating system issues a read or write command to the virtual disk attached to the VM.

2. A SCSI command is issued to the SCSI driver for the virtual disk and then the virtual SCSI controller processes the command.

3. The virtual SCSI controller forwards the command to the **VMkernel**.

4. The VMkernel does the following:
    - Locates the VMDK file on the VMFS volume that the VM is attempting to read or write to
    - Maps the SCSI command to the block on the virtual disk
    - Maps the block on the physical disk to the block that corresponds to on the virtual disk
    - Builds and sends a SCSI command with the true physical block location on the VMFS datastore

5. The HBA installed on the ESXi host, packages the SCSI command into a Fibre Channel packet.

6. The HBA transmits the command to the SAN.

7. A SAN switch or the SAN itself receives the request and ensures that it is process appropriately.

Fibre Channel storage arrays

Fibre Channel storage arrays generally come in two flavors: single and dual controller storage arrays.

Single controller storage arrays

Single controller storage arrays are the easiest to understand and configure. The single controller is responsible for all the reads and writes to the attached disks. Storage array shelves are attached to the controller with P2P Fibre Channel connections. Some storage arrays will connect to the single controller using dual FC connections. Single controller storage arrays can withstand FC link failures when configured correctly but are unable to withstand controller failures. If a single controller storage array needs a firmware update or to fix a problem with the storage controller, the whole array must be taken out of production duty. VMware storage **vMotion** can be utilized to migrate data off the single storage array when planning for an outage. Unfortunately, in the case of an unplanned outage, we may end up with stranded data on the storage array. With VMware View we must do a rebalance operation in order to migrate the virtual desktops of the storage array.

Dual controller storage arrays

Dual controller Fibre Channel storage arrays are inherently more highly available. In the event of a storage controller failure or FC port failure, the backup storage controller can take control of the connected disks and storage shelves. We can perform maintenance on a single controller without taking down the whole array. Individual storage shelves must be connected to both storage arrays, and consult with your vendor for the appropriate wiring diagram for your arrays.

Dual controller Fibre Channel storage arrays are typically found in the following varieties:

- **Active-Active storage system**: LUNs presented by the storage controller can be accessed from either storage controller. The Active-Active setup in some cases this improve throughput to disks due to more processing power being available to handle SCSI commands. All paths available to an Active-Active setup are available for use for SCSI commands. Note that some storage processors perform more slowly in Active-Active due to state synchronization than in Active-Passive. Consult with your storage vendor to determine the best configuration available for your storage environment.

- **Active-Passive storage system**: In an Active-Passive setup, the storage processors are configured such that each LUN is assigned to a single storage processor. If multiple LUNs are serviced by the set of storage processors the passive controller for one LUN may be configured as the active controller of another LUN providing some load balancing. SCSI commands for a LUN sent to the passive storage processor will fail as the passive storage processor is not servicing that LUN. In the event of a failure, the passive storage processor will take over from the active storage processor. The ESXi host will automatically choose Fibre Channel paths to the active storage processor for each LUN.

- **Asymmetrical storage system**: An Asymmetrical storage system supports **Asymmetric Logical Unit Access (ALUA)**. ALUA-compliant storage systems provide varying levels of access for each port attached to the SAN environment. This system can be thought of as an Active-Passive system, but where the passive partner can still service SCSI traffic for traffic it doesn't own. This is typically accomplished by forwarding the traffic onto the active storage processor for the LUN.

Fibre Channel and SAN requirements for VMware ESXi

VMware ESXi has certain requirements for a SAN network to function reliably and with the best performance:

- SAN storage hardware should be on the VMware Hardware Compatibility list.
- Only one VMFS volume per LUN.
- For machines that boot locally from directly attached storage, do not set up a diagnostics SAN LUN.
- For diskless server a diagnostics SAN LUN should be set up and shared between the servers.
- For multipathing, each LUN must present the same LUN number to all hosts.
- Ensure that enough queue depth is available from the physical HBA during system setup. See your vendor for more information regarding HBA queue depth or refer to the *vSphere Troubleshooting* documentation.
- On Microsoft Windows systems, increase the SCSI timeout value to 60. This allows Windows to better tolerate failover scenarios and Fibre Channel path switching.

 The VMware hardware compatibility guide can be found at: http://www.vmware.com/resources/ compatibility/search.php

ESXi Fibre Channel and SAN restrictions

ESXi doesn't support all Fibre Channel devices and all Fibre Channel situations.

ESXi has the following limitations:

- ESXi does not support Fibre Channel tape drives or devices.

- You cannot use multipathing software from within a VM to a single physical LUN. You can, however, attach multiple disks to a VM and use software technologies such as Microsoft Windows dynamic disk or disk mirroring/ RAID technologies such as **Logical Volume Manager** (**LVM**) or **MDADM** on Linux or **GEOM** on **Berkeley Software Distribution** (**BSD**) systems.

- Do not mix Fibre Channel HBAs from different vendors on a single host. A single LUN cannot be accessed from different model HBAs, which can increase the failover time of Fibre Channel paths and storage processors.

- Ensure the firmware of the HBAs, storage processors, and Fibre Channel switches are all up to date. Most support requests can be avoided if the firmware is upgraded as a first step in troubleshooting.

- 16 GB FC HBAs are supported but there is no support for end-to-end 16 GB connectivity. To get full bandwidth, create two 8 GB connections from the switch to the storage array.

Planning for High Availability

Fibre Channel is designed from the ground up to be highly available. Fibre Channel can be set up with redundant pairs of fibre to the host without a significant effort. Storage arrays with redundant controllers are readily available and can be failed over seamlessly.

Planning for High Availability with Fibre Channel switches

Fibre Channel switches can be utilized to provide a networked and redundant storage environment. When planning for high availability we always want to deploy a redundant pair of switches. Each host should be set up with dual port Fibre Channel HBAs. In this configuration, we connect the first HBA to the first switch and the second HBA to the second switch. Storage arrays are also hooked up in a similar manner with fibre running to both switches. Single controller storage arrays should come with two Fibre Channel connectors that can be used for this purpose. The following diagram is a scenario where a single switch has failed:

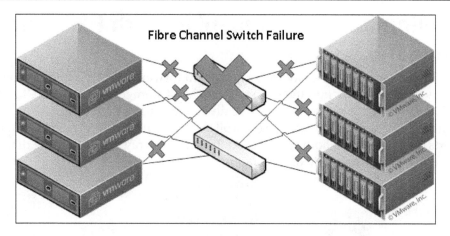

Here we see that half the links have gone down due to the failure. Note that the second switch has taken over the remaining SAN traffic duties.

With dual controller Fibre Channel storage arrays, we want to hook each controller into a different switch. If each controller has a second Fibre Channel port, then we would hook both controllers into both switches. In the event of an individual FC port or fibre failure, the storage controller will failover to either the other available Fibre Channel switch or other storage controller. The following diagram is an example of a single storage controller failing in a dual controller storage array:

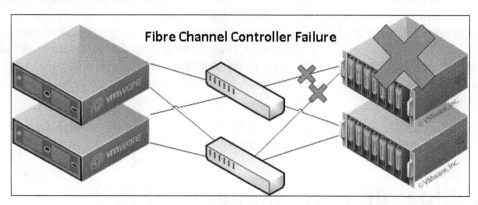

Pending on the configuration and vendor the second storage controller will take over the SAN traffic. Consult your vendor documentation for high availability of storage arrays.

Planning for high availability with P2P Fibre Channel

With P2P Fibre Channel, we have a fairly straight forward task. We want to hook each server redundantly into the storage array. Most storage controllers are limited to two FC connections per controller. Usually that means in this configuration we are hooking a single server into a single controller storage array. Simply connect both FC ports on the server to both FC ports on the storage array. The following diagram shows a P2P Fibre Channel with link failure:

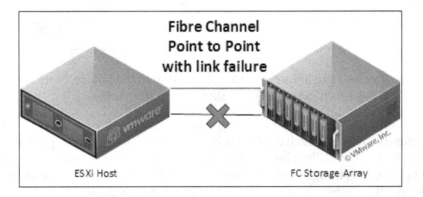

For two servers with a single controller storage array, we would hook each server to a single port on the storage array. Unfortunately, there is not a Fibre Channel port failover scenario in this configuration as there is only a single FC connection available. A failure of the Fibre Channel port requires taking the host out of the cluster or into maintenance mode to continue working. We can use VMware HA and VMware view in configurations outlined in other chapters to provide HA in this configuration.

For dual controller storage arrays, we can hook two servers to the storage array in a redundant manner using both FC ports on both FC controllers.

Multipathing and managing Fibre Channel from within VMware vSphere Web Client

When configuring multipathing it is useful to be able to check on the paths available for each HBA. To do so, we need to do the following:

1. Log into vSphere web client.

2. Navigate to the host with the HBA we are inspecting.

3. Navigate to **Manage | Storage | Storage Adapters**.

4. Select the HBA that we want to check the paths on.

5. Select **Paths** in the **Adapter Details** section.

6. Here we can see all the paths available to the one storage processor as well as the LUNs the storage controller is presenting:

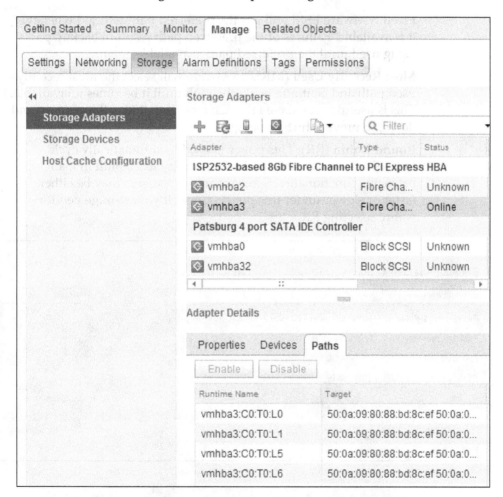

To configure the multipathing policy, we need to do the following:

1. Log into vSphere Web Client.

2. Navigate to the datastore we want to configure the multipathing policy on.

3. Navigate to **Manage | Settings**.

4. Select **Connectivity** and **Multipathing** from the left column.

5. Select the host we want to change or view the multipathing policy on.

6. For High Availability, verify every host has two or more paths available.

7. To change the multipathing policy select **Edit Multipathing...** in the right side of **Multipathing details**.

8. We have the following multipathing options:

   ° **Fixed**: VMware ESXi will use the preferred path selected whenever it is available. Failures of the preferred path result in backup paths being used until the preferred path is available again.

   ° **Most Recently Used (MRU)**: VMware will select the most recently used path and continue using the path until it becomes unavailable. This is useful if you have Fibre Channel link that is flapping up and down, to prevent further outages.

   ° **Round Robin (RR)**: This policy is used to automatically cycle through all the available paths. This policy has a built in load balancing functionality. Some storage processors may be either faster or slower under this policy. Consult your storage vendor before selecting RR.

Fibre Channel checklist

To ensure the maximum amount of uptime in your production environment, the following steps outline general failover cases that you should account for, as well as common failure or degradation scenarios that can be avoided:

- Ensure your Fibre Channel storage controllers, HBAs, and hosts have the latest firmware.

- Document Fibre Channel zoning, storage controllers, switch, server and HBA configurations, and topologies.

- Only change the path policy of a multipathed Fibre Channel SAN if you understand the implications of the change and that it aligns with your storage vendor's best practices.

- Verify that the Fibre Channel HBA is installed in a PCI slot that is rated for that speed.

- Document all portals/management access for the SAN infrastructure.

- Document access and security restrictions if applicable.

- Avoid changing the LUN IDs of any datastore in use by VMware.
  The change in LUN ID will likely result in an outage on that datastore.
  Rescan the HBAs/VMFS datastores to detect the new LUN ID.

- Check with your storage processor vendor for best practices and configurations for use with your VMware ESXi environment.

Fibre Channel High Availability checklist

The following is the Fibre Channel High Availability checklist:

- Power off each host, verify the other hosts can power on the VMs that were attached to the powered off host.

- Create and manually verify the topology map of your Fibre Channel infrastructure.

- Check that each host can survive a single Fibre Channel path failure.

- Verify each host has multiple paths to all storage processors.

- Power off each SAN switch in the cluster, verify the hosts failed over and can still power on VMs.

- Determine if redundant Fibre Channel cards are required. This can prevent a FC HBA failure from knocking out your host.

- Verify that you still have access to any management tools for the storage controller in the event of an outage. Consider hosting any required management tools on a separate cluster or physical machine.

- Verify that you still have access to any management tools for VMware products in the event of a Fibre Channel outage. Consider hosting any required management tools on a separate cluster or physical machine.

- Ensure that all LUNs have a unique ID across your SAN infrastructure.

- Ensure that all hosts in the cluster can see all LUNs on the SAN. This is essential for host failover to function.

- Ensure backups of all Fibre Channel storage arrays are taking place. Pay close attention to your vCenter server, view servers and view base images.

Summary

In this chapter, we learned about high availability with Fibre Channel SAN. We covered normal failure scenarios, ways to build a redundant SAN network, and the differences and technologies available for Fibre Channel High Availability. We covered the workflow and protocol basics of Fibre Channel and how they affect your environment. We also covered best practices and zoning so that our environment can be made reliable and secure.

In the next chapter, we will cover High Availability for networking, NFS, and iSCSI. We will tackle our failover scenarios and best practices to keep your environment's networking in tip top shape.

7

NFS, iSCSI, and Network Planning

VMware Horizon View has a heavy reliance on the network infrastructure to be able to consistently deliver a good user experience. This means any network infrastructure we intend to use with VMware Horizon View will need to be highly available as well. We will cover the network resources used by Horizon View and the HA strategies for each network resource.

In this chapter, we will cover the following topics:

- Active Directory
- DNS
- DHCP
- Network High Availability
- VMware vSphere ESXi networking
- VMware VMkernel configuration
- Switching
- NFS
- High Availability for NFS
- iSCSI
- High Availability for iSCSI

Active Directory

Active Directory is one of the corner stones of VMware Horizon View. We utilize Active Directory for user authentication, user groups and assignments, service accounts, and in most cases managing authentication against our vCenter. Active Directory is hosted on Microsoft domain controllers. In many environments, the domain controllers also double as DNS and DHCP servers.

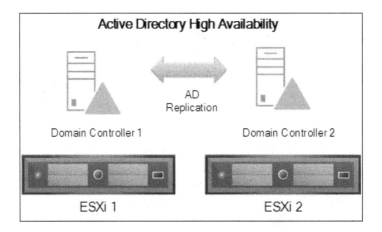

Active Directory should be deployed such that we can guard against a single host failure. We can do this by deploying two or more domain controllers. Domain controllers will mirror the data of other domain controllers in the same domain. Due to the inherent redundancy of domain controllers, we can install the domain controller on local disk on each host or on shared storage available to the ESXi cluster. When domain controllers are deployed on shared storage, ensure that DRS rules are configured to keep the domain controllers on separate hosts.

DNS

DNS servers are essential for both virtual desktops and VMware Horizon View clients. For High Availability, we will want to deploy two or more DNS servers, and configure the clients and servers with the two DNS servers deployed. DNS servers should be kept on separate hosts. This can be accomplished by storing the VM on local disk or with DRS anti-affinity rules. DNS can often be deployed on the same server, that is, our domain controller. Only the largest environments will have to split the two up for performance reasons. There are several types of DNS servers available that can be used, but the best practice is to use Microsoft DNS servers integrated into our Active Directory environment.

Active Directory-integrated DNS servers

In most cases of View deployments, we will utilize our Domain Controllers as DNS servers. In this situation, the DNS entries are updated when the Domain Controllers replicate the Active Directory data.

Microsoft DNS servers can be installed from the Add or Remove role wizard, which is available from the Microsoft Server Manager.

DNS Servers should be configured with "Allow only secure dynamic updates" in order to ensure that DNS entries are not hijacked. To configure secured dynamic updates, perform the following steps:

1. Launch the DNS Manager.
2. In the console tree, right-click on the applicable zone and click on **Properties**.
3. Navigate to the **General** tab and check whether the zone is **Active Directory-integrated**.
4. In the **Dynamic updates** section, click on **Secure only**.

The best practice for Microsoft DNS servers is to enable **Zone Aging/Scavenging**. This option is available under the **General** tab of the DNS Zone properties. When the DNS server removes entries that haven't been renewed in several days/hours, it is known as DNS Scavenging. The scavenging threshold is configurable.

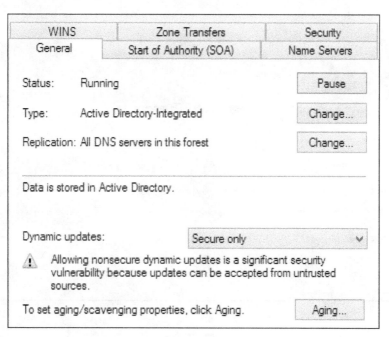

DNS Zone Properties

Here, we choose to set the aging and dynamic updates to **Secure only.**

DHCP

DHCP is a must have in VMware Horizon View environments as your virtual desktops, thin clients, zero clients, and software clients will all depend on IPs being served by a DHCP server. DHCP servers can be configured in multiple ways, but as best practice it is advisable to configure the DHCP server to utilize a subnet dedicated to View servers and virtual desktops. For Microsoft DHCP servers, it is recommended to configure name protection on the DHCP scope to prevent DNS hijacking and mischief.

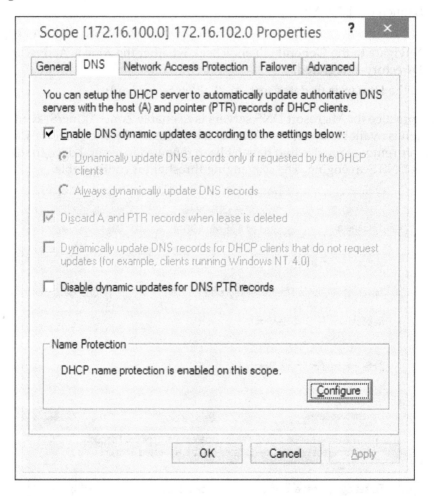

DHCP High Availability

DHCP High Availability can be configured in multiple ways to handle failure scenarios and load balancing. In all high availability scenarios, ensure that the two or more DHCP servers are on separate hosts. We can accomplish this by storing the DHCP server on local disk or with DRS anti-affinity rules. DHCP servers are often hosted on domain controllers as the resource requirements are quite low. DHCP needs to be separated from the domain controller role in the largest environments only.

- **Active/Backup**: In this mode, we configure a primary DHCP server to handle all the DHCP traffic on the network. The backup node will receive DHCP state information but will not handle any DHCP traffic while the primary is active. Once the primary DHCP server fails, the backup takes over. This can be accomplished with server clustering solutions such as **Windows Server Failover Cluster (WSFC)** or by using Windows Server 2012's built in DHCP clustering.

> For non-Microsoft DHCP servers, consult your vendor's documentation for configuration details.

- **Active/Active**: In this mode, we configure both servers to operate simultaneously serving the same IP range. The DHCP servers will sync their state such that one can operate in the event of a failure. In Microsoft DHCP server, this is called "Load sharing mode" and it is available in Windows Server 2012. This provides the highest possible performance and redundancy.

> To configure an Active/Active DHCP server, check out your vendor documentation.

- **Split Scope**: In this mode, two DHCP servers are operating independently of each other, controlling a split of the IP ranges available on the subnet. As an example, Server A could be servicing 10.0.0.10 to 10.0.0.128 on a 24 subnet and Server B could be serving 10.0.0.129 to 10.0.0.254. Split Scope configurations are available for most DHCP server implementations. When configuring split scope, ensure that both servers are serving the same DHCP options to ensure that clients are consistently configured. This is especially important when dealing with VoIP phones and some zero or thin clients.

DHCP clustering can be configured from the DHCP management tools. Simply right-click on the existing DHCP scope and select **Configure Failover...**. You can select a partner server to participate in the cluster and the load balancing and availability method you need.

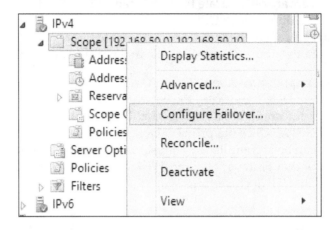

 For more details about DHCP server High Availability, visit https://technet.microsoft.com/en-ca/library/ hh831385.aspx?f=255&MSPPError=-2147217396.

Network High Availability

When dealing with networking, we tend to arrive at the same solutions for high availability for both NFS and iSCSI. We must configure redundant links and redundant switches for both NFS and iSCSI to survive a single link or switch failure.

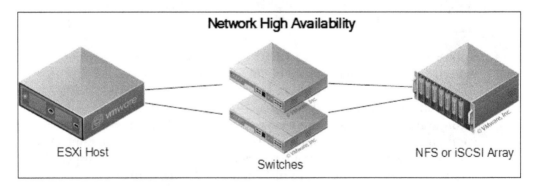

The previous example has a redundant pair of switches configured to protect against a switch failure. We have links going from all ESXi Hosts connecting to two separate switches. Each NFS or iSCSI storage array has a link to each switch, thus forming a redundant pair.

Switching

Switching in a VMware vSphere ESXi environment doesn't vary significantly from other highly available environments. We want to configure a redundant pair of switches to handle any switch failures that may occur and to handle any single link, NIC, or port failure that can occur. Pairs of redundant switches should be built such that they can share traffic between them. ESXi may present VMs on different NICs and (in some cases) will need to send traffic between them over a Switch interconnect. This is especially true in environments with two or more ESXi hosts.

In switching environments where **Spanning Tree Protocol (STP)** or a variant of STP is enabled, we want to ensure that our ESXi hosts and our storage systems are plugged into ports where Portfast is enabled. STP with Portfast disabled works by monitoring the traffic on the port for STP topology and MAC addresses on it to determine if any network loop exists in the topology. STP moves through the following states when a port becomes active:

- **Blocking**: In this state, the port does not participate in forwarding packets onto other network ports. The port is only listening for STP and topology packets (**Bridge Protocol Data Units** or **BPDU**). No MAC address processing occurs in this state. Ports end up in a Blocking state if STP determines that transmitting packets on the port would result in a network loop. Blocking ports will move to the the Listening state frequently to determine when to unblock the port.

- **Listening**: In this state, the port does not participate in forwarding packets onto other network ports. During this state, the port is only listening for STP and BPDU packets. The port may move into the Learning state if it is determined the port won't cause a network loop. Otherwise, it moves back to the blocked state.

- **Learning**: All user traffic is still blocked but we are now learning the attached MAC addresses on the network and updating the MAC tables. It will quickly move on to the Forwarding state.

- **Forwarding**: The port is functioning as a normal network port and forwarding traffic. BPDU traffic continues to be monitored and this port may move into a Blocked state if STP determines this port may cause a loop.

To ensure that an ESXi host is not temporarily blocked in the event of a failover or vMotion, we want the STP protocol to put ESXi into the Learning and Forwarding states right away via the Portfast enabled setting. This will prevent packets from being dropped from the VM perspective when vMotioning between hosts or during host failures. Note that Portfast will not prevent network loops as quickly as STP and should only be enabled on trusted ports such as ESXi hosts and storage hosts.

If jumbo frames are being enabled, verify they are supported end to end and that all devices attached are configured for jumbo frames. Protocols such as iSCSI and NFS benefit from the higher data transfer rates of jumbo fames and the reduced processing time. If your switch supports it, enabling flow control Rx at the switching level can prevent congestion problems and reduce iSCSI traffic retransmits.

Where possible, dedicated switches for storage communications provide higher reliability due to simpler configuration requirements and a lower chance of having congestion issues.

Storage High Availability

Generally storage vendors will have their own documentation and methods for configuring storage appliances for High Availability. In general, we want to ensure that the following is configured on each storage device:

- Two or more physical NICs wired into two or more switches
- Choose storage solutions with High Availability or failover options
- For load sharing, use multiple IPs to allow separate traffic pathways to utilize multiple links
- Configure storage with RAID 6 or RAID 10 to ensure that any disk failures will not result in corruption or data loss during the rebuild phase
- For Virtual SAN, we want to ensure that multiple NICs on each host are dedicated to Virtual SAN traffic
- Storage should be kept on its own isolated network
- When configuring jumbo frames, be careful when adding new hosts to the network as they may not be able to communicate if misconfigured

VMware vSphere ESXi

To ensure High Availability for vSphere ESXi, we want to make sure that two NICS are available to every vSwitch or Distributed Switch, with an exception when multipathing with iSCSI. We also want to consider the load balancing policy we use and how it affects the traffic distribution.

For vSwitches, do the following:

1. Log into the vSphere Web client.
2. Navigate to the host we are managing the networking for.
3. Select the **Manage** tab and then select **Networking**.
4. Select **Virtual switches** on the right-hand side column.
5. Highlight the virtual switch and select the **Edit Settings** button.
6. The load balancing policy is found under the **Teaming and failover** section.

For distributed switches, do the following:

1. Log in to the vSphere Web client.
2. Navigate to the Network view.
3. Find the vSwitch in the navigation tree on the left-hand side of the page.
4. Select the **Manage** tab and select the **Settings** sub-tab.
5. Select **Polices** and then click on **Edit....**
6. The load balancing policy is found under the **Teaming and failover** section.

On the vSwitch or distributed switch **Edit Settings** page, we can see the configuration of the adapters and how they will behave in a failure scenario.

In the following example, we have vmnic0 and vmnic1 configured on the same vSwitch. When multiple adapters are placed in the **Active adapters** group, the NICs will be used simultaneously to provide bandwidth according to our load balancing policy. In the event of a failure, the remaining working NICs in the **Active adapters** group will take over and service traffic.

If we wanted to configure the NICs with an Active/Backup scenario, we would move one or more NICs into the **Standby adapters** group, ensuring at least one or more NICs was in the **Active adapters** group. In this scenario, if all of the active adapters fail the NICs in the **Standby adapters** group will be activated. A normal use case for this scenario is if our NICs operate at different speeds. For example, if we had two 10 Gbps NICs and 2 Gb onboard NICs in our server, rather than only depending on the 10 Gbps network, we could include the Gb NICs as backups in case our whole 10 Gbps network went down. This provides additional levels of redundancy.

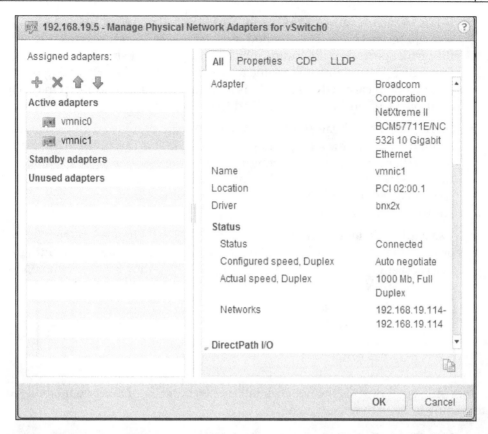

Unused adapters are NICs not assigned to any vSwitch. The distribution of traffic on the vSphere NICs are governed by the load balancing policy of the vSwitch or distributed switch. We have the following options:

- **Route based on the originating port ID**: We use the virtual port ID of the vNIC on the vSwitch or distributed switch to determine which physical NIC will be used for sending or receiving VM traffic. This is the default policy for all new virtual switches and is the least prone to failure or error. There are no special switch requirements for this load balancing method.

- **Route based on IP hash**: This selects an uplink based on the hash of the source and destination IP address of each packet. Non-IP packets simply sample the bytes where the IP fields would normally be stored. The IP hash method cannot be used with Beacon Probing. This method requires that switches be configured with EtherChannel on the ESXi ports.

- **Route based on source MAC hash**: This selects the upload based on the source Ethernet hash. This method uses the VM MAC address instead of the virtual port ID to determine which physical NIC it should be routed to. In practice, this is almost the same as "route based on the originating port ID", except in cases where the VM is a router or load balancer that may have multiple MAC addresses or MAC address spoofing.

- **Route based on physical NIC load**: The VMs are monitored and balanced based on the load they are putting on the NICs. This can result in higher multipath performance, but it might come at the cost of more CPU time from the ESXi host. If an uplink remains busy at 75 percent or higher for 30 seconds or more, the host will move part of the VM traffic to another physical NIC with free capacity.

- **Use explicit failover order**: This uses the NIC that is highest in the NIC order, which is not in a failure state. This policy reduces the bandwidth of the ESXi server to that of the single NIC in use. This policy is not recommended.

> More details about VMware load balancing can be found at http://kb.vmware.com/selfservice/microsites/search.do?language=en_US&cmd=displayKC&externalId=2006129.

Another important point is the network failure detection. We have two methods for determining if the network is down:

- **Link Status Only**: This relies on the NIC link status to determine if we can route traffic. This is the simplest method of failure detection but doesn't address common network failures such as:
    - Physical switch ports blocked by STP or incorrect VLAN configuration
    - Link failure to an upstream switch, gateway, or datastore

- **Beacon Probing**: This sends out and listens for beacon probes on all NICs in the switch or distributed switch. It uses the success or failure of these beacons to determine if the link has failed. In the event of a link failure, the beacon on the link will fail and will be put into standby until the beacon succeeds again. This method is best used in vSwitches or distributed switches with three or more NICs as then the Beacon successes and failures can determine if a single link has failed, based on the quorum.

The next option, **Notify Switches**, determines the NIC ARP behavior in the case of a failover or vMotion of a VM. This option should be left at the default **Yes** unless you have unusual use cases such as Microsoft Network Load Balancing in unicast mode.

Failback determines if we will go back to using an active NIC that has previously failed or to continue to use the standby NIC. This should be left to **Yes** in case the standby port is undesirable for use for any reason. Leaving it as **No** is useful in case you have a poor quality link that is flapping up and down, as it will prevent multiple failovers and failbacks. NFS best practice is to set the failback setting to **No**.

VMkernel configuration

When configuring vSphere ESXi to utilize NFS or iSCSI, we must pay special attention to the configuration of the VMkernel adapter.

For iSCSI, we can bind the VMkernel port to be used with iSCSI. This is available under the **Edit VMkernel** settings after the software iSCSI is enabled. Hardware solutions will always use the physical NIC or HBA that is configured. For iSCSI solutions, it is preferable to have 1 NIC bound to each VMkernel port used for iSCSI. This enables multipathing failover between the VMkernel ports using the iSCSI protocol. This allows iSCSI to manage the traffic flow from each adapter.

For NFS, the VMkernel will use the following criteria to determine which VMkernel adapter to use for NFS:

- It will use the first VMkernel adapter that is on the same subnet as the NFS server; if multiple adapters are on the subnet, it will use the first one found
- If no VMkernel adapters exist on the same subnet, NFS will be sent out the first VMkernel adapter enabled for management traffic and will traverse the default gateway (undesirable)

NFS does not benefit or load balance from multiple VMkernel adapters. If link aggregation is needed, we should configure a VMkernel adapter on a vSwitch or distributed switch with multiple active adapters.

NFS

NFS, specifically NFSv3, as VMware uses it, is a network protocol for accessing files over the network. It allows a remote server to share files with a client. In the case of VMware, we are accessing the various VMware files on a remote data store. VMs are stored on the remote datastore in VMX, VMDK files, and various log, cache, and configuration files.

NFSv3 operates on UDP. UDP protocols do not inherently have a retransmit or packet drop detection in place. As such, we need to ensure our NFS network is reliable and free of packet loss. NFS will retransmit lost packets but will at least double the latency of file operations. The UDP protocol allows NFS to operate with minimal overhead and performance loss over the network.

NFSv3 has the following network requirements:

- Reliable local network free of packet drops
- Fast local network (at least 1 Gbps, ideally 10 Gbps)
- Low latency (in the ideal case, no more than one or two network hops away)
- ESXi hosts should be on the same subnet as the NFS storage
- NFS ports must be allowed past the firewall on the NFS server
- NFS server must allow the IP addresses of all ESXi hosts in the cluster
- NFS traffic must be separated (VLAN or physically) from regular network traffic, as it is unencrypted and not authenticated
- Server NICs should be on the VMware **Hardware Compatibility List (HCL)**

VMware stores all VMs on the NFS server in thin provision format. This reduces the amount of storage used and allows for more VMs to share the same datastore. In the case of VMware Horizon View, it can provide significant storage reductions on thick/full-provisioned VMs. Note that NFS servers should always be monitored for overcommit and total remaining storage. When used with VMware Horizon View, overcommit on a datastore can be substantial in the range of 2-3x of the total space available.

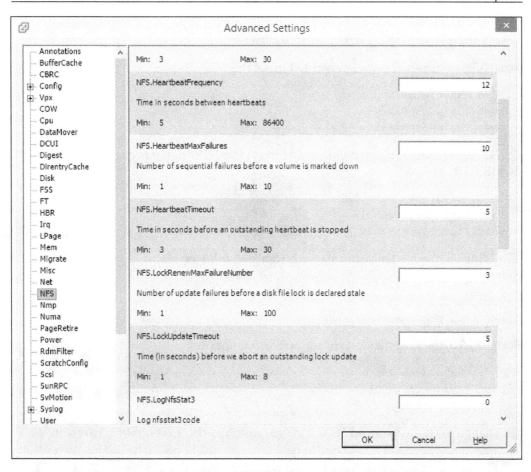

For best performance, we can tweak the NFS settings on the ESXi hosts. The settings can be found under ESXi server advanced settings. To edit advanced configuration options, select the ESXi/ESX host in the inventory panel and navigate to **Configuration | Software | Advanced Settings** to launch the settings window. The following setting changes are suggested:

```
NFS.HeartbeatFrequency = 12
NFS.HeartbeatTimeout = 5
NFS.HeartbeatMaxFailures = 10
```

These settings improve the performance of VMware HA and reduce failure and failover times in outage scenarios.

TCP/IP heap size should be tweaked up when we start getting a large number of datastores connected via NFS to an ESXi host.

For 8 NFS volumes, it is recommended to set the TCP/IP heap to 6 MB / 30 MB:

```
NFS.MaxVolumes=8
Net.TcpipHeapSize=6
Net.TcpipHeapMax=30
```

For 32 NFS volumes, it is recommended to set the TCP/IP heap size to 24 MB / 120 MB:

```
NFS.MaxVolumes=32
Net.TcpipHeapSize=24
Net.TcpipHeapMax=120
```

 For ESXi 5.5, the host maximums for NFS are as follows:

```
NFS.MaxVolumes=256
Net.TcpipHeapSize=32
Net.TcpipHeapMax=512
```

For ESXi 6.0, the host maximums for NFS are as follows:

```
NFS.MaxVolumes=256
Net.TcpipHeapSize=32
Net.TcpipHeapMax=1536
```

All changes to the Advanced ESXi configuration require a reboot to take effect.

> See the VMware KB article for more details: http://kb.vmware.com/selfservice/search.do?cmd=displayKC&docType=kc&docTypeID=DT_KB_1_1&externalId=2239

NFS third-party features

NFS storage appliances often offer advantages over normal NFS storage solutions. This can range from simple manageability improvements to storage deduplication and various snapshot and backup technologies. Replication is often a capability of NFS storage appliances, which will allow you to survive site failures.

Deduplication

NFS vendors can offer de-duplications, which reduce the storage requirements even further. Deduplication finds duplicate patterns in the VMDK files and reduces the number of copies physically stored. Deduplication is very useful when combined with VMware Horizon View. View full-provisioned desktops can be deduplicated with a high degree of storage reduction as much as 75 percent. View thin-provisioned won't see as high a reduction ratio, since the base image is only stored once. However, with careful planning, deduplication can allow you to hit higher consolidation ratios of both virtual servers and desktops.

Backups and snapshots on NFS

NFS datastores often include backup and snapshot features that allow you to quickly backup and restore your VMs. An NFS volume snapshot can be quickly mounted onto the ESXi hosts and allows you to boot or copy the old VMs off the snapshot. NFS snapshots pending on the vendor may be even more granular allowing individual VM backups and restores to happen instantly. Consult your storage vendor for more details about the backup technologies available to you.

NFS High Availability

NFS technology is fundamentally dependent on the local network to operate. Any highly available NFS implementation must also account for the possibility of single failures in the network. This is outlined in the *Network High Availability* section.

It should be noted that the VMkernel on the storage network should be set up on a switch or distributed switch with multiple NICs available. This will ensure the VMkernel on the storage network always has access to the NFS server in the event of a link failure.

It is best practice to have a VMkernel on the same subnet as the NFS server as there is no port binding available to NFS. NFS traffic is sent out according to these rules.

- It will use the first VMkernel adapter that is on the same subnet as the NFS server. If multiple adapters are on the subnet, it will use the first one found.

- If no VMkernel adapters exist on the same subnet, NFS will be sent out the first VMkernel adapter enabled for management traffic and will traverse the default gateway (undesirable).

NFS does not benefit or load balance from multiple VMkernel adapters. For link aggregation, the VMkernel adapter should be configured on a vSwitch or distributed switch with multiple active adapters. NFS requires the load balancing policy to be configured to use multiple NICs in an active/active scenario. Without configuring the load balancing policy, NFS will be limited to the speed of the fastest NIC; however, with multiple NFS shares on different IPs it is possible to utilize multiple links to achieve higher throughput. This configuration is not true load balancing but is often referred to as load sharing. Depending on your performance requirements, it may provide adequate bandwidth to the ESXi hosts.

NFS can be used with "Route based on IP hash", provided the switches support EtherChannel. This requires multiple IPs to be configured on the storage solution.

NFS can be used with the "Route based on physical NIC load" load-balancing policy.

 Check out the VMware NFS best practices for more details: http://www.vmware.com/files/pdf/VMware_NFS_BestPractices_WP_EN.pdf

iSCSI

iSCSI is a protocol designed to transmit SCSI commands over the network. Like regular SCSI devices, the protocol is designed to interact with datastores on a block level. VMware treats iSCSI devices like any other block device presented to the vSphere hosts.

There are two main ways to interact with an iSCSI storage device: hardware and software iSCSI adapters. Here's a brief description of each:

- Hardware iSCSI adapters are add-on cards added to the host or embedded in the network adapter of the host. iSCSI adapters present the host with an HBA that can be used to write data to attached disks. Hardware iSCSI adapters have the advantage of higher performance and lower latency over software iSCSI adapters but may require special drivers or out of band or command line configuration.

- A software iSCSI adapter is a software stack that interacts with iSCSI storage datastores over the NICs attached to the vSphere host. Software iSCSI adapters come standard with the VMware vSphere kernel and can be used with any vSphere host. Software adapters can be configured from within the vSphere client or vSphere Web client.

iSCSI is based on top of TCP and as such can be limited by some of the performance issues that are associated with TCP. TCP in general requires more CPU time to process compared to UDP protocols and can be limited by network cache size. Network cards with **TCP offload engine (TOE)** functionality can improve the speed of iSCSI connections.

Network congestion is a major concern with iSCSI as the SCSI protocol doesn't deal with network latency well. Best practice for iSCSI traffic is to dedicate any 1 Gbps NICs to iSCSI, and ensure bandwidth is dedicated for iSCSI traffic on 10 Gbps NICs.

VMware vSphere currently doesn't support any of the authentication or encryption methods that iSCSI normally supports unless it is tied into a hardware HBA solution. iSCSI traffic should always be isolated either via VLAN or physical separation from regular user and server traffic.

Like Fibre Channel, iSCSI operates with the SCSI protocol in mind. The storage array will present LUNs to the host which will then be formatted in VMFS format. ESXi hosts read and write to the iSCSI datastore like it was any other VMFS datastore.

iSCSI concepts

Let's examine the terminology that will be encountered when dealing with iSCSI:

- **Names**: iSCSI nodes have globally unique names independent to the network adapters attached or assigned IP addresses. iSCSI names have three different naming conventions:
  - **Extended Unique Identifier (EUI)**: The EUI naming convention begins with the prefix "eui." and is followed by a 16 character name. The Name consists of 24 bits for the manufacture company name and 40 bits for a unique ID.
  - **iSCSI Qualified Name (IQN)**: The IQN is a unique string of characters up to 255 characters long that describe the host. This takes the form **"iqn.yyyy-mm.naming-authority:unique name"**.
    - yyyy-mm: This is for the year and month of the date the naming authority was established, for example, 1998-01.
    - naming-authority: This is the Internet domain of the naming authority in reverse order, for example, com.vmware.iscsi.
    - unique-name: This is an arbitrary name of the storage device that can be set by the network or storage administrator.
  - **iSCSI Alias**: This is an easy-to-remember name that can be used instead of the iSCSI qualified name. These names are not unique and are simply available for convenience.

- **IP addresses**: Like all network devices, the iSCSI targets and clients must be configured with an IP address on the local subnet. It is best practice to keep iSCSI traffic on its own physical network or VLAN to keep the traffic secure.

- **iSCSI Initiators**: iSCSI initiators are hosts or devices that consume data. In a VMware vSphere environment, your ESXi hosts will be the iSCSI initiators. These initiators can either be hardware- or software-based, as outlined previously.

- **iSCSI Targets**: iSCSI targets are hard drives, disk arrays, tape drives, or datastores that are accessed via iSCSI. In a vSphere environment, you will mostly be using iSCSI targets as datastores for VMs.

- **iSCSI Session**: It is a TCP connection between an iSCSI Initiator and iSCSI target. Multiple sessions can originate and terminate at each initiator or target. Many sessions can be used for redundancy, load balancing, and link aggregation.

- **iSCSI Portal**: iSCSI nodes track all the session between the target and initiator. A portal manages all the IP and TCP mappings. Portals will track what iSCSI names are in use or available (IQN, EUI, or Alias). iSCSI Portals can be thought of as the equivalent of Fibre Channel Paths.

- **Logical Unit Number (LUN)**: The SCSI protocol operates based on LUN numbers to identify storage devices on the network. Any LUNs presented by Storage providers should be unique to the SAN network.

iSCSI High Availability

iSCSI is fundamentally dependent on the local network in order to remain functional. We must design and build our networking infrastructure to avoid single points of failure. As such, the *Network High Availability* section is a prerequisite for iSCSI high availability.

For high availability in an iSCSI environment, we want to avoid NIC teaming and instead use multiple VMkernel ports on vSwitches that are assigned single NICs. After enabling iSCSI on the VMkernel port, the iSCSI protocol will use the multiple VMkernel ports in a multipathing scenario. It is possible to use iSCSI with NIC teaming. However, we must ensure that port security is disabled on the vSwitch ports used for iSCSI traffic. We cannot use Multipathing if iSCSI is enabled on only one VMkernel.

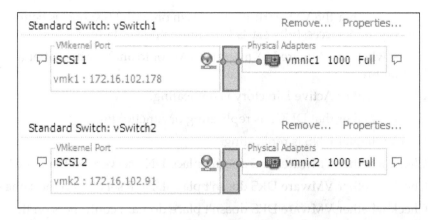

Multipathing provides us with multiple paths to the storage array permitting iSCSI to rapidly deal with link or path failures. After the VMkernel is set up with multipathing, we can manage the iSCSI paths from the iSCSI HBA properties. See the Fibre Channel section on multipathing for more details.

 See the VMware article on iSCSI for more details:
http://www.vmware.com/files/pdf/iSCSI_design_deploy.pdf

Failure testing checklist

Every good cluster should be failure ready. As part of testing, I've provided a checklist to run through to verify the configuration and good standing of any View HA environment.

Note that the loss of a View connection server will disconnect any connected sessions, but the View client should be able to restart the session on the other View connection server after it reconnects.

Run through each step and check whether VMware Horizon View is still working and can service new logins:

- Power off each DNS server, one at a time.
- Power off each DHCP server, one at a time, and check whether DHCP addresses are still being allocated.
- Power off each domain controller, one at a time.
- Check whether each ESXi host is configured to power on after a power loss.

- Check whether the VM startup/shutdown on each ESXi host is being followed and successfully starts VMs after a power failure.
- Check whether VMware HA migrates VMs onto another host after a host failure.
- Check whether Active Directory is replicating.
- Check whether that DHCP is replicating or functioning.
- Check whether DNS is replicating.
- Check whether VMware DRS doesn't place DNS servers on the same host.
- Check whether VMware DRS doesn't place DHCP servers on the same host.
- Check whether VMware DRS doesn't place domain controllers on the same host.
- Check whether the DNS round robin is working via `nslookup`.
- Document High Availability procedures for NFS.
- Document High Availability procedures for iSCSI.
- Document High Availability procedures for DNS.
- Document High Availability procedures for DHCP.
- Document High Availability procedures for domain controllers.
- Train other systems administrators about View HA procedures.
- Take a break. Your VMware Horizon View servers are walk away safe.

Summary

In this chapter, we successfully configured and deployed VMware View in a highly available cluster. We covered software requirements, network requirements, and hardware requirements. We also discussed the topologies available to us to deploy highly available services.

In the next chapter, we will explore monitoring and notification solutions for VMware Horizon View. We will cover things to look for when trouble arises and how to quickly recover from common failures.

8
Monitoring VMware Horizon View

VMware Horizon View deployments are dependent on adequate monitoring and performance checking. In this chapter we will explore the various methods of gathering information from VMware View and how to use that information to improve the availability of the environment and performance.

In this chapter we will cover:

- How to monitor the View connection servers
- How to monitor the VMware vSphere server
- Monitoring tools available
- VMware vRealize Operations Manager for Horizon View
- Monitoring checklist

Monitoring the View connection servers

VMware Horizon View comes with a built-in dashboard for quickly assessing the status of the services involved in the View infrastructure. You can access the dashboard from the administrator's console, available at `https://your.server.fqdn/admin/#/dashboard`.

The dashboard quickly shows you any problems that are preventing your View environment from functioning.

Common errors shown are:

- Certificate errors for connection server
- Connection server offline

- Event database offline or not configured
- Security servers offline
- Security server certificate error
- View composer offline
- View composer certificate errors
- ESXi hosts offline
- vCenter servers certificate error
- vCenter offline
- Datastores offline
- Domain controller unreachable

There is a **System Health** dashboard that provides links to View, vSphere, and various other components, as shown below:

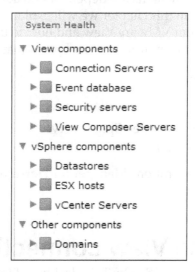

In addition to **System Health**, there is the mini dashboard, which is available in all views in the top-left corner of the screen:

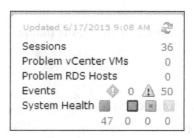

On this dashboard we can see at a glance:

- The number of current sessions
- The number of problem virtual desktops
- The number of problem remote desktop server hosts
- The number of errors and warning events that have happened in the last two days
- A summary of the system health and problem system

View Event database

For issues that are not immediately apparent, there is an event log. This is an optional setup step when setting up a View connection server. It is highly recommended to have the event log installed and configured. The event log requires a Microsoft SQL server or Microsoft SQL Server Express, or an Oracle database to operate. The database must be set up with network access, a username, and a password in order to create and edit tables on the database. The Event Configuration settings are available under the **View Configuration** menu in the left column.

The event log is available at `https://your.connection.server.fqdn/admin/#/event`, as you can see in the following figure:

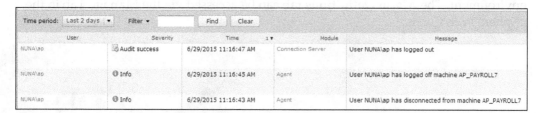

User	Severity	Time	1 ▼	Module	Message
NUNA\ap	Audit success	6/29/2015 11:16:47 AM		Connection Server	User NUNA\ap has logged out
NUNA\ap	Info	6/29/2015 11:16:45 AM		Agent	User NUNA\ap has logged off machine AP_PAYROLL7
NUNA\ap	Info	6/29/2015 11:16:43 AM		Agent	User NUNA\ap has disconnected from machine AP_PAYROLL7

The event database will contain details about user logins, warnings about virtual desktop failures, and notifications about resource outages. Error messages will be generated for View composer failures, including recompose events and refresh events. This is the first line of information gathering when troubleshooting issues with VMware Horizon View.

Monitoring the VMware vCenter server

VMware vCenter comes with a comprehensive set of alarms for monitoring VMs, datastores, and ESXi hosts. The alarms can be found under the **Alarms** tab in the vSphere Client, and under the **Monitor** tab of the vSphere Web Client.

Alarms are available for each host, datastore, VM, and vCenter server. Alarms are aggregated into the larger containers such as a data center, cluster, resource pool, and folder, and can be used to quickly check the alarms of all contained objects.

The alarms can be viewed in the vSphere Web Client via the **Monitor | Issues** tab. The **Issues** tab lists all the issues that the environment currently has. You can also see a history of the triggered alarms in the **Events** tab.

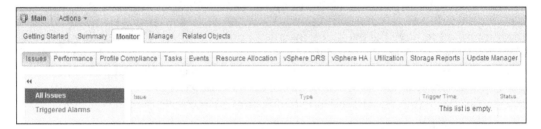

There is a list of alarm definitions that can be altered, enabled, or disabled to suit the environment. The **Alarm Definitions** tab can be accessed via the **Manage** Tab in the vSphere Web Client.

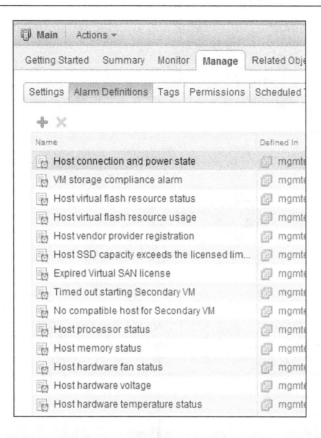

Using the alarm definitions, you can define actions that occur when each alarm is triggered. Common actions include rebooting a troublesome server/application that has a memory leak if the RAM usage gets above a certain amount, sending an email or SNMP trap if the alarm is triggered, and running scripts against the host or VM when an event is triggered.

Unfortunately, a complete guide to vSphere/vCenter monitoring is beyond this book, but please read up on the subject in VMware's documentation.

For more details about VMware vSphere monitoring, visit:
`http://pubs.vmware.com/vsphere-60/topic/com.`
`vmware.ICbase/PDF/vsphere-esxi-vcenter-server-60-`
`monitoring-performance-guide.pdf`

Monitoring tools available

Here we will examine the available tools for VMware-related monitoring. We will cover tools available from VMware and select third parties.

Horizon View Event Viewer

VMware has provided a tool for View Event monitoring, this tool monitors your View event database and will send out e-mails when warnings or errors are found. This tool is one of the quickest ways to know when there is a problem with your view environment. Unfortunately, at the time of writing, this tool is not set up to run as a service and must be run with a logged in account.

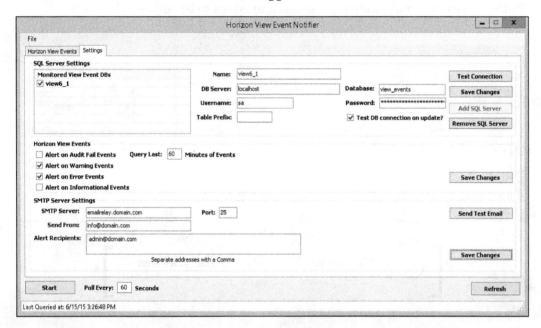

Horizon View Event Notifier can be found on VMware's website: `https://labs.vmware.com/flings/horizon-view-event-notifier`

RVTools

RVTools is a freeware tool made by Rob de Veij. It will log into the vSphere host or vCenter host and will provide a neatly formatted table of nearly every aspect of the virtual environment. In particular, it is very good at discovering unnecessary snapshots, unnecessary CDs attached to VMs, low disk space, outdated tools, and unused VMDK files on the datastore. RVTools provides a rapid health check feature that will discover configuration problems and issues to be addressed.

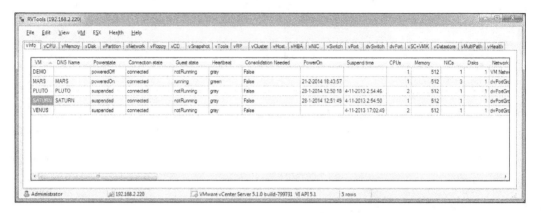

 RVTools can be found on Rob de Veij's site: `http://www.robware.net/`

PCoIP Session Statistics Viewer

The PCoIP Session Statistics Viewer is a handy tool for rapidly graphing PCoIP session details, and allows you to quickly troubleshoot image quality, latency, and packet loss issues with Horizon View sessions.

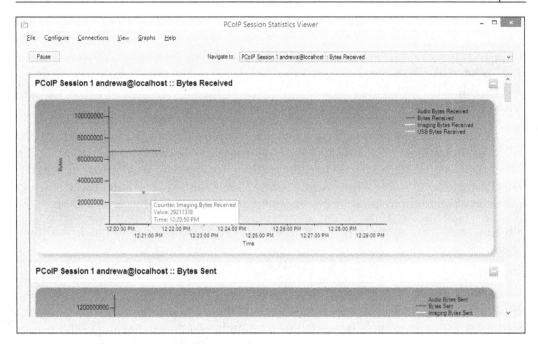

The PCoIP Session Statistics Viewer is available at the Teradici support website (requires free account registration):

`https://techsupport.teradici.com/ics/support/`
`DLRedirect.asp?fileNum=424&deptID=15164`

vRealize Operations Manager for Horizon View

vRealize Operations for Horizon is the most comprehensive monitoring solution available for VMware Horizon View allowing complete end-to-end monitoring of the environment. It was formerly known as the vCenter Operations Management Suite.

vRealize will collect metrics about:

- RAM usage
- Login times
- Outages
- Disk performance

- Disk latency
- Disk usage
- CPU times
- Capacity planning

VMware vRealize also has the capability of performing a rapid root cause analysis and troubleshooting from one dashboard. The vRealize dashboard is designed to provide a quick look at the health of the environment, providing an easy-to-read Green-Yellow-Red color scheme for the conditions of the various VMware assets. vRealize comes complete with auto-correlation logic that will intelligently alert administrators to changes in the environment and weed out non-relevant alerts.

vRealize can also monitor trends in the environment's growth and usage. In addition to growth monitoring, it can monitor VMs for wasted resources and make VM hardware recommendations. This will allow you to get the best performance out of the existing resources.

vRealize Operations for Horizon is an add-on to the standard vRealize Operations Manager Suite, and as such, is dependent on having an operational and licensed vRealize Operations Manager VM up and running. vRealize Operations Manager is available in three varieties: Windows, Linux, and Virtual Appliance. For the sake of simplicity, in this book, we will assume you are using Virtual Appliance.

>
> For more information on vRealize Operations Manager for Horizon View, visit:
>
> `https://www.vmware.com/support/pubs/vcops-view-pubs.html`
>
> For more information on vRealize Operations Manager visit:
>
> `https://www.vmware.com/support/pubs/vrealize-operations-manager-pubs.html`

vRealize Operations Manager Virtual Appliance installation

There are a few steps required before we can get a functional vRealize Operations Manager for Horizon View running. Note that while free trials are available from VMware, the product is a licensed product. Consult with your VMware reseller for pricing information.

First we must install the vRealize Operations Manager and configure it.

1. Log into `http://my.vmware.com` and download all the items from the *vRealize Operations Manager for Horizon View* section. In particular, you will need:

   - `vRealize-Operations-Manager-Appliance.ova` (vRealize Operations Manager Virtual Appliance)

   - `VMware-vrops-viewadapter.pak` (plugin for Horizon View for vRealize)

   - `VMware-v4vbrokeragent.exe` (View Broker for connection server)

   - `VMware-v4vdesktopagent (x86 or x64).exe` (vRealize Desktop Agent for Horizon View), which is included by default in the View Agent install in version 5.2+ and 6.0+

2. Configure a set of domain user credentials for vRealize Operations Manager with which to log into vCenter and Horizon View.

3. Grant the vRealize user Administrator privileges on the vCenter server using the vSphere Client or vSphere Web Client.

4. Grant the vRealize user administrator privileges on the Horizon View connection server using the `https://your.server.fqdn/admin/#/administrator` web page.

5. Log into the vCenter Server via the vSphere Client or vSphere Web Client.

6. Deploy the vRealize Operations Manager OVA.

7. On the **OVF Template Details** screen, select **Next**.

8. Accept the **End User License Agreement** and select **Next**.

9. Enter the **Name** and **vCenter Location** for the VM, then select **Next**.

10. Select the deployment configuration size and select **Next**.

11. Select the storage location and click **Next**.

12. Select the network for the Virtual Appliance to use, then select **Next**.

13. Enter the **Timezone, Default Gateway, DNS, Network 1 IP Address**, and **Network 1Netmask**. Record the network details for future use. Select **Next**.

14. Wait for the OVF appliance to deploy.

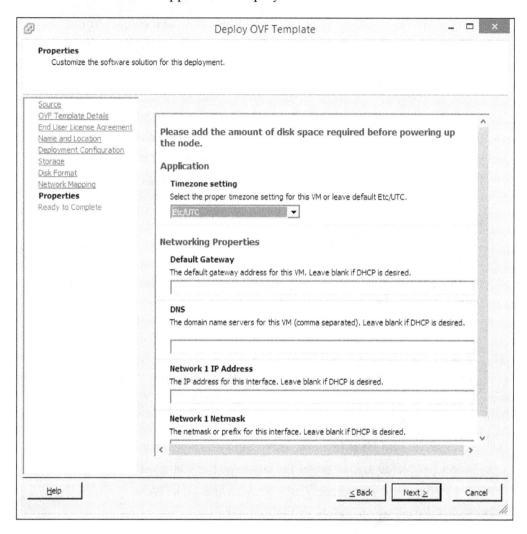

 For more information about installing vRealize Operations Manager, visit: http://pubs.vmware.com/vrealizeoperationsmanager-6/ topic/com.vmware.vcom.core.doc/GUID-FB728744-8847-4BFA-9FEF-EA485307A4B7.html

vRealize Operations Manager Configuration

Next we will configure the vRealize Operations Manager Virtual Appliance.

1. Log into the IP of the Virtual Appliance you provided in step 10 of the previous section.

2. Select **Express Installation**.

3. On the **Getting Started** screen, select **Next**.

4. Enter a password for the admin account and select **Next**.

5. On the **Ready to Complete** page, select **Finish**.

6. Wait for the setup to complete.

7. On the **vRealize Operations Manager Configuration** Screen, select **New Environment** under **Choose Configuration**. Select **Next**.

8. Accept the **End User License Agreement** and select **Next**.

9. Enter the product key or select **Product Evaluation**. Hit **Next**.

10. On the **Ready to Complete** screen, select **Finish**.

11. On the **Solutions** screen, select the add solution button (green plus button).

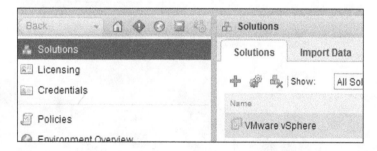

12. Upload `VMware-vrops-viewadapter.pak` to vRealize Operations Manager.

13. Select **Next**.

14. Accept the **End User License Agreement** and select **Next**.

15. Select **Finish** after the add-on is installed.

16. On the **Solutions** page, select the **VMware Horizon** option.

17. From the toolbar, select configure (2 gray gears).

18. Select **vCenter Adapter**.

19. Add an instance of the vCenter Adapter using the green plus sign.

20. Enter the **Display name, Description, vCenter Server FQDN,** and enter administrator credentials for the vCenter Server.

21. Test the connection and accept the certificate.

22. Save the settings.

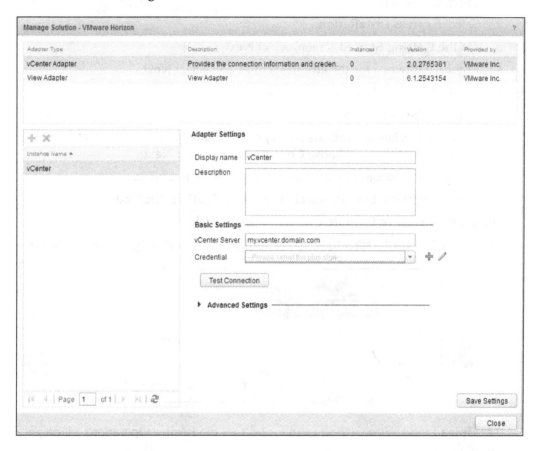

23. Select **View Adapter**.

24. Add an instance of the View Adapter using the green plus symbol.

25. Enter the **Display name, Description, Adapter ID,** and **Credential**.

26. Test the connection.

27. Save the settings.

28. Close the **Manage Solution** window.

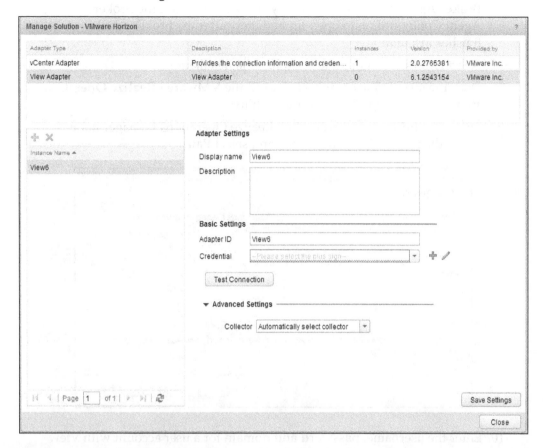

Install the VMware vRealize Operations View Broker Agent

We will now install and configure the View Broker Agent on the View connection server. Note that installation of the Broker on a security server is not possible.

1. Using the console or remote desktop, log into the View connection server.

2. Download the VMware-v4vbrokeragent.exe file to a local temporary location on the View connection server.

3. Launch the VMware-v4vbrokeragent.exe file with administrator privileges.

4. Select **Next**.

5. Accept the **End User License Agreement** and select **Next**.

6. (Optional) Select the **Launch the VMware vRealize Operations View Broker Agent configuration utility** checkbox to cause the Broker Agent Configuration to open immediately after the broker agent finishes installation.

7. Select **Install** then **Finish** to complete the installation.

8. Once the installation completes, launch the **VMware vRealize Operations View Broker Agent Configuration** utility.

9. Enter the address and port of the vRealize Operations Manager node. Leave the port as the default **3091**, and select **Pair**.

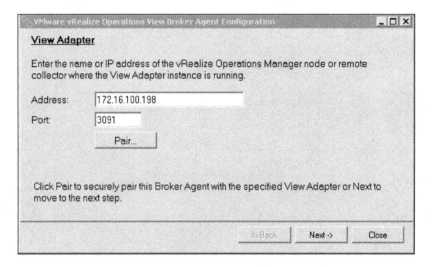

10. Enter the username, password and domain for a user account with View Connection Server administrator privileges, and select **Validate...** to validate the credentials. Then select **Next**.

11. Enter the username and password for the Event database, you may need to consult with your DBA for the details. The account requires read access to all the View Event database tables. Select **Validate...**, then **Next**.

12. Enter the **View Pool Filter**. By default, all the pools are monitored, but that can be filtered down. Select **Validate...** if you opted not to monitor some of the pools. Select **Next**.

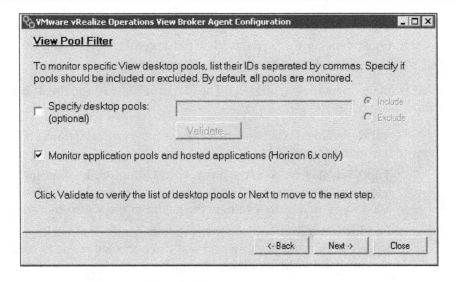

13. Review the details and select **Finish**.

Installing the vRealize Operations for Horizon Desktop Agent

If you are using VMware Horizon View 5.0 or 5.1, the vRealize Operations for Horizon Desktop Agent does not come installed by default with the View Agent. As such, the agent must be installed separately. As of the writing of this guide, View 5.0 and 5.1 have several outstanding troublesome bugs that are resolved in View 5.2 and 6.0. I would strongly urge the reader to consider a View Environment upgrade rather than to bother with installing the vRealize Operations for Horizon Desktop Agent.

For details on the procedure, view the VMware vRealize Operations for Horizon Installation document, available on VMware's site:

```
http://pubs.vmware.com/vrealizeoperationsmanager-6/
topic/com.vmware.ICbase/PDF/vrealize-horizon-61-
installation-guide.pdf
```

vRealize Operations Manager Dashboard

vRealize Operations Manager for Horizon View has several reports and dashboards available to quickly assess the state of the View environment.

Navigate to **Home** to view the dashboards. The Horizon View plugin by default loads several dashboards for use.

- **View Overview**: This dashboard displays the most critical details about your View environment.

  ○ **Top View Alerts**: Here the most critical issues with your Horizon View infrastructure and Virtual Desktops are displayed. This widget allows you to rapidly evaluate the health of the View environment.

  ○ **Pod Indicator Metrics**: This widget displays the Pod health, Pod workload number of connected and disconnected sessions, and various bandwidth and latency details.

  ○ **View Pods**: Lists the pods in the View cluster.

  ○ **Pod Session Metrics**: Details the sessions with the View connection server and how many of each type of session is active.

  ○ **Pod Capacity Metrics**: Details the capacity used and available to the View environment.

- **View Infrastructure**: Details the status of the ESXi hosts and any underlying hardware for the VMware Horizon View environment.

  ○ **View Infrastructure Hosts**: Details the current status of the workload of each ESXi host.

  ○ **View VDI Desktop VMs**: Shows the status of the desktops in View.

  ○ **View Datastores**: Shows the status of the View datastores.

  ○ **View RDS Hosts (View 6.0)**: Shows the status of the RDS hosts attached to the View 6.0 or higher environment.

- **View Users**: Details the users and sessions that are ongoing in the View environment.

  ○ **View Sessions**: Lists the objects involved in the View environment. Selecting an object from the View Sessions window will cause the other widgets to display the sessions related data.

  ○ **Session Related Objects**: Creates a graph of the resources used by the object selected in the View sessions widget. Includes resource pool, host, network, and datastore.

- ° **Object Metrics**: Lists the metrics available to the object in a tree view. Expand the individual nodes to view individual metrics. Selected metrics are graphed on the Object Metric Charts.
- ° **Object Metric Charts**: Lists the health of the object selected and lists the metrics selected from Object Metrics.
- ° **Object Alerts**: Lists the current alerts for the object.

- **View Remote Sessions**: Details the current sessions of VDI desktop sessions, RDS desktop sessions, and application sessions. It breaks down the sessions by PCoIP latency, TX bandwidth, and TX packet loss.
    - ° *** Sessions**: Lists the sessions of each type.
    - ° **Top * Session PCoIP Latency (ms)**: Lists the latency of each session.
    - ° **Top * Session PCoIP TX Bandwidth (kbit/s)**: Lists the bandwidth being used for transmitting the session. We can use this to identify users with high requirements, or ones who may be streaming video, audio, or doing 3D work in their session.
    - ° **Top * TX Packet Loss (%)**: We can use this to identify weak links in our network infrastructure by analyzing sessions that are experiencing packet loss.

- **View VDI Pools**: Details the resources of each pool and object broken down by View pool.
    - ° **VDI Desktop Pools**: Selects a pool from this widget to populate the other widgets with stats.
    - ° **VDI Desktop Pool Indicator Metrics**: Lists the various statistics for the pool, and the overall health of the pool. This gives relative performance metrics and details about the capacity of the pool.
    - ° **VDI Desktop Pool VMs**: A quick colorized block chart of the resource allocation of the VMs in the pool. The colors represent the VMs' health.
    - ° **VDI Desktop Sessions**: Lists the sessions of the VDI pool.
    - ° **Various Top * Details**: Several widgets that present the top usage and latency graphs of the various VMs.

- **View RDS Pool**: Similar to the VDI pools view, this view lists all the details about the RDS pool sessions and applications available.
    - ° **Farms**: Lists the RDS farms configured on the View connection server.
    - ° **RDS Desktop Pools**: Lists the RDS pools configured on the View connection server.

- ° **Application Pools**: Lists the application pools configured on the View connection server.

- ° **Various Drill Down Views**: You can see various statistics and performance details about all the farms, RDS pools and application pools available in the View environment.

- **View TS Pools**: Lists the Terminal Services desktop pools configured on the View connection server. Like RDS pools, this lists all the metrics for terminal services.

- **View Applications**: Lists the various View application pools' health and statistics.

- **View Desktop Usage**: Lists the number of sessions and events with a timeline graph of when each event and session happened.

- **View Remote Sessions**: This dashboard breaks down the statistics for the remote sessions:

  - ° **View Remote Sessions**: Lists the remote sessions taking place.

  - ° **Session Indicator Metrics**: Lists the metrics of the current session.

  - ° **Session Logon Breakdown**: Lists the logon time for the session.

  - ° **Session Processes**: Lists the processes being run by the user.

  - ° **Session Health & Events**: Lists the events that have occurred in the session.

- **View RDS and TS Host Details**: Lists the various statistics for RDS and TS hosts.

- **View Adapter Self Health**: Lists the adapters' health.

- **Recommendations**: Lists the recommendations that can improve the health and performance of the environment. As a new feature, the vRealize Operations Manager can automatically make recommended changes to the environment with user approval. Recommendations include CPU usage, disk usage, and various efficiency changes.

- **Diagnose**: This tab provides a rapid aggregation of objects to determine what may underlie a failure of a VM. This View will show the datastores, host, network, and resource pool that the VM belongs to, as well as the health rating of each asset.

- **Self Health**: This outlines the health of the vRealize cluster.

Monitoring checklist

Depending on the way you choose to monitor VMware Horizon View, you may respond to outages in different ways. Please make sure to document how you monitor each event, and ensure you receive a timely notice to respond to the issue. After each step, ensure that a notice was received and that you can respond to each issue quickly.

- Power off each host one at a time
- Induce a high RAM usage situation on one or more VMs
- Induce a low disk space situation on a View desktop
- Induce a low disk space situation on a Horizon View server
- Induce a low disk space situation on a datastore being used by the Horizon View environment
- Shutdown each View connection server one at a time
- Shutdown each Active Directory server one at a time
- Shutdown each DNS server one at a time
- Unplug an Ethernet cable from an ESXi host
- Unplug a power cable from an ESXi host
- Shutdown a datastore and verify the outage notification (CAUTION: do in test environment only) and have a good backup ready
- Verify disk failures of the ESXi host cause notifications
- Verify disk failures on the attached datastores cause notifications
- Monitor the performance of the PCoIP sessions and verify enough bandwidth exists in the environment
- Monitor the CPU performance of the ESXi hosts
- Monitor the RAM usage of the ESXi hosts
- Monitor the RAM usage of the guest VMs
- Monitor the disk usage of the ESXi host
- Monitor the IOPs of attached disks
- Monitor the network usage
- Log into a virtual desktop and stop the View Agent
- Verify virtual desktops in an error state cause notifications

Summary

In this chapter, we learned about the various monitoring options for VMware Horizon View. We went through the basic ways to gain insight into VMware Horizon View and the various monitoring solutions available for Horizon View. We learned how to install vRealize Operations Manager for Horizon View, and we learned about the various resources we can use to log and monitor the performance of the VMs and hosts.

In the next chapter, we will go over upgrade and downtime planning for VMware Horizon View, and cover the best practices for minimizing outages.

Upgrade and Downtime Planning

9

Every production environment goes through iterations and changes. Upgrade and downtime planning is an essential part of keeping an environment running efficiently. This chapter will run you through the basics of a Horizon View upgrade and the various things to plan for during the upgrade and migration.

We will cover the following topics for upgrading VMware Horizon View:

- Prerequisites and common pitfalls
- The upgrade order and plan for vCenter
- The upgrade order and plan for Horizon View
- Host upgrade planning
- Storage upgrade planning
- Network upgrade planning

Prerequisites and common pitfalls

It's critical to check your environment end to end for compatibility issues prior to upgrading VMware Horizon View. Unfortunately, VMware has made Horizon View product incompatibilities easy to stumble across if the prerequisite documents are not studied before an upgrade. The version numbers do not imply compatibility with Horizon View. For instance, Horizon View 5.1 was not compatible with the first release of vCenter 5.1 when it came out.

For more details about VMware product interoperability visit the matrix webpage at `http://partnerweb.vmware.com/comp_guide2/sim/interop_matrix.php`.

When upgrading VMware Horizon View, a vCenter upgrade is commonly accompanied.

Note that there is a specific order and compatibility requirements when upgrading vCenter and its various accessory products.

In particular, the following order should be followed when upgrading Horizon View and vCenter:

1. vCenter SSO (if external)
2. View Composer
3. View Connection Servers
4. vCenter Server
5. ESXi hosts
6. vShield NSX Edge
7. vShield App
8. vShield Endpoint
9. VMware Tools
10. View agent
11. View clients

The following KB details all the steps for a successful vCenter upgrade:

`http://kb.vmware.com/selfservice/microsites/search.do?language=en_US&cmd=displayKC&externalId=2109760`

For more details regarding View Upgrades, I highly recommend reading the VMware Horizon View 6.0 upgrades guide:

`https://pubs.vmware.com/horizon-view-60/topic/com.vmware.ICbase/PDF/horizon-view-60-upgrades.pdf`

View Composer 6.0

The View Composer is the first component to be upgraded in any upgrade scenario. The View Composer is typically collocated with the vCenter Server but may be on its own server/VM.

The View Composer upgrade can be performed without an outage but will disable recomposing while the environment is being upgraded. For full provisioned desktops, no new desktops can be created. For thin-provisioned desktops refresh after logoff, recomposing, and rebalancing will not be possible during the upgrade scenario.

For outage planning, it is best to upgrade the View Composer just ahead of the outage window. This will give you a shorter total outage time. Plan for a 15-minute outage of the View Composer while the upgrade is underway.

The requirements for the View Composer 6.0 and for the View 6.0 upgrade are as follows:

- Windows Server 2008 R2, 2008 R2 SP1, or 2012 R2
- The server must be 64-bit
- The server can be Standard or Enterprise licensed
- 1.4 GHz CPU or faster with two CPUs
- 4 GB of RAM or higher
- 40 GB or more disk space
- Microsoft SQL Server 2008 (R2 SP2 or SP3), 2012, or 2012 SP1 (x86 or x64) (Express, Standard, Enterprise, or Datacentre)
- Oracle 10g R2 or 11g R2
- Administrative privileges for the vCenter, View Security Servers, and or separate View Composer server

The steps for upgrading the View Composer are as follows:

1. Download the desired View Composer from https://my.vmware.com/. Copy the executable to the server/VM that you wish to install it on.
2. Take a snapshot of the VM with the View Composer or otherwise confirm you have a working backup. Make sure the vCenter and View Composer SQL database is included in the backup.
3. If you are upgrading from View 5.0.x or earlier, ensure that you have a certificate installed (that is trusted by the clients) on the View Connection Server.

4. Make a copy of the folder that contains SSL certificates. This folder is located at `%ALLUSERSPROFILE%\Application Data\VMware\VMware VirtualCenter`.

5. For all linked-clone desktop pools, log into the View Administrator console and disable provisioning on the virtual machines.

6. If any desktops are set to refresh the OS disk on logoff, set the **Refresh OS disk on logoff** setting to **Never**.

7. If any pools or desktops are scheduled for a recompose, rebalance, or refresh, those tasks must be cancelled before the upgrade.

8. Launch the View Composer executable on the desired server/VM. Often, this component is collocated with the vCenter Server.

9. Follow the installer's step by step instructions to install the component. Additional information can be found in *Chapter 1, VMware Horizon View 6.0 Connection Server HA*, about View Composer installation. Or in the official VMware Horizon View installation document.

10. Specify whether you want the wizard to upgrade the database schema. The recommended action is yes. If you select no, you will have to manually update the schema using the SviConfig command line tool. View the Horizon View upgrade document for more details about manual schema upgrades.

11. When the wizard prompts for the View Composer port number, select the default port number 18443.

12. For all linked-clone desktop pools, log into the View Administrator console and enable provisioning on the virtual machines.

13. If any desktops are set to refresh the OS disk on logoff, set the **Refresh OS disk on logoff** setting to **Always**.

View Connection Server 6.0

The VMware Horizon View Connection Server represents the hearts and brains of the View environment and will take up the bulk of the outage window to upgrade.

The View Connection Servers have the following requirements:

- Windows Server 2008 R2, 2008 R2 SP1, or 2012 R2
- The server must be 64-bit
- The server can be Standard or Enterprise licensed

- 1.4 GHz CPU or faster with two CPUs
- 4 GB of RAM or higher
- 40 GB or more disk space
- The View Composer should be upgraded before the View Connection Server
- An SSL certificate that is trusted by the clients and installed on each View Connection Server

Plan 15 to 30 minutes of outage time for each connection server you have.

For more details about installation of the View Connection Server, please read through *Chapter 1, VMware Horizon View 6.0 Connection Server HA*, which includes screenshots and step by step instructions.

The steps for upgrading the View Connection Server are as follows:

1. Download the View Connection Server from `https://my.vmware.com/` and copy the executable to each View Connection Server.
2. For all linked-clone desktop pools, log into the View Administrator console and disable provisioning on the virtual machines.
3. Take a snapshot of all View Connection Servers. Or take a backup of the View Connection Servers that includes the LDAP database.
4. Ensure that all local mode desktops are checked in. Remove all transfer servers prior to upgrade (For upgrades from View 5).
5. In the View Administration interface, navigate to **View Configuration | Servers**.
6. Select the **Security Servers** tab and select the first View Security Server.
7. Click on **More Commands | Prepare for Upgrade or Reinstallation**.
8. Click on **OK**.
9. Repeat steps 5 through 7 for all of the View Security Servers.
10. Launch the installer on each View Connection Server. Follow the steps to install or upgrade the View Connection Server.
11. Repeat for each View Connection Server.
12. Launch the installer on each View Security Server. Follow the steps to install or upgrade.
13. Verify the status of the View Composer, vCenter, and View Security Servers from the View Administration console.

VMware vCenter Server 6.0 for Windows

VMware vCenter is the next component to upgrade in our VMware Horizon View upgrade. vCenter doesn't need to be upgraded with every Horizon View upgrade but needed when upgrading between major versions.

It is strongly recommended to consult the interoperability matrix prior to a vCenter upgrade.

Note that components other than vCenter need to be considered. VMware vCenter needs to be upgraded with its co-depended products. Common co-dependent products include vShield, SRM, NSX networking, Operations Manager, vRealize, and so on.

Depending on the complexity of the environment, plan for a 1 to 4-hour outage of the vCenter for the upgrade.

VMware vCenter 6.0 has the following requirements:

- At least 17 GB of free space
- 10 GB of RAM for up to 10 hosts and 100 VMs
- 18 GB of RAM for up to 100 hosts and 1000 VMs
- 26 GB of RAM for up to 400 hosts and 4000 VMs
- 34 GB of RAM for up to 1000 hosts and 10,000 VMs
- Windows Server 2008 SP2 or newer
- One of the following supported databases:
    - MS SQL Server 2008 R2 SP2 or newer, must be Standard or Enterprise edition. Express edition is not supported.
    - PostgreSQL (supports up to 1,000 hosts and 10,000 virtual machines).
    - Oracle 11g and Oracle 12c.

VMware vCenter is only required for managing hosts and for commanding the recompose, refresh, provisioning and rebalance operations. As such, if we can find a window where we don't require recompose, refresh, provisioning, and rebalance operations we can upgrade the VMware vCenter without interrupting the View environment. Note that the vCenter we are upgrading to must be compatible with the installed Horizon View environment.

For vSphere 6.0 upgrades, please consult the vSphere upgrade guide prior to performing the upgrade:

`https://pubs.vmware.com/vsphere-60/topic/com.vmware.ICbase/PDF/vsphere-esxi-vcenter-server-60-upgrade-guide.pdf`

For vCenter upgrade best practices, visit VMware's KB article on upgrade procedures:

`http://kb.vmware.com/selfservice/microsites/search.do?language=en_US&cmd=displayKC&externalId=2109772`

The steps for upgrading the vCenter are as follows:

1. Download the latest compatible vCenter from `https://my.vmware.com/` and copy it to the vCenter VM or host.

2. Ensure that all the ESXi hosts in the environment are ESXi 5.0 or later.

3. Take a snapshot of the vCenter Server or a backup that includes a SQL or Oracle backup of the database. This should include a snapshot of the View Composer database, Single Sign-On database, and vCenter database.

4. Upgrade the vCenter Single Sign-On component.

   ° If the Single Sign-On component is an externally deployed on an external Single Sign On server, upgrade that server to Standalone Platform Services Controller.

   ° Internal vCenter Single Sign-On will be upgraded to an embedded Platform Services Controller deployment as part of the vCenter installation.

5. Launch the vCenter installer on the vCenter Server.

6. Select install the vCenter Server for Windows.

7. Complete the installation steps and accept the license agreement.

8. Enter the vCenter Administrator credentials; for single sign on this should be `administrator@vsphere.local` and the corresponding password.

9. Click on **Next**.

10. Configure the Platform Services Controller:

    ○ If the Single Sign-On Server is collocated with the vCenter Server configure Platform Services Controller and click on **Next**. The installer will migrate the Single Sign-On service to an embedded Platform Services Controller.

    ○ If the Single Sign-On Server is installed on another server, ensure it has been upgraded to the external Platform Services Controller. Enter the information for the external Platform Services Controller and click on **Next**.

11. Configure ports 80 and 443 such that they are free for the Platform Service Controller. Click on **Next**.

12. Configure the install, data, and export directories and select **Next**.

13. Review the summary page and select **Upgrade**.

14. Click on **Finish**.

VMware vCenter Server 6.0 Appliance

As of writing this guide, the vCenter Server appliance is not commonly used with VMware Horizon View. The main downside to the appliance is the inability to collocate the View Composer with the vCenter as the View Composer requires a Windows Server. As a consequence of that the main benefit of one reduced Windows Server license isn't fulfilled when using the appliance with Horizon View. VMware does support using the vCenter appliance with Horizon View, but with using a standalone View Composer Server.

For information on upgrading the vCenter Server Appliance, please consult VMware's documentation:

```
https://blogs.vmware.com/vsphere/2015/09/updating-
vcenter-server-appliance-6-0-to-update-1.html
```

For upgrading from the vCenter Appliance 5.5 to 6.0 please read the following documentation:

```
https://pubs.vmware.com/vsphere-60/index.
jsp?topic=%2Fcom.vmware.vsphere.upgrade.doc%2FGUID-
66836F60-A095-4749-86C9-1DAFB5D21070.html
```

VMware Update Manager

VMware Update Manager is the next upgrade on our list. Update Manager is one of the fastest methods to manage and upgrade the ESXi hosts that our View environment relies on. The Update Manager is not critical to the Horizon View environment or the vCenter environment and can be upgraded at any time after the vCenter upgrade.

The Update Manager is usually co-installed on the vCenter Server.

Follow these steps to upgrade the Update Manager:

1. Stop the Update Manager service, and take a backup of the Update Manager database.
2. Launch the Update Manager installer on the vCenter Service. The Update Manager installer is included in the vCenter Installer.
3. Select an installer language and click on **OK**.
4. On the upgrade warning message screen, click on **OK**.
5. On the welcome screen, click on **Next**.
6. Accept the license agreement, click on **Next**.
7. Select whether to download updates from the default download location.
8. Select whether to delete the old update files. Click on **Next**.
9. Enter the vCenter credentials the update manager will use.
10. Type the Update Manager credentials that it will use to authenticate against the vCenter Server. Click on **Next**.
11. Enter the Update Manager database credentials. Click on **Next**.
12. On the database upgrade page, select **Yes, I want to upgrade my Update Manager database** and **I have taken a backup of the existing Update Manager database**. Click on **Next**.
13. Specify the Update Manager port settings and any applicable proxy settings, and select **Next**.
14. Click on install to begin the upgrade.
15. Click on **Finish**.

ESXi 6.0 upgrade planning

In this guide, we will assume that the Upgrade Manager is being used for the ESXi upgrades.

Typically, with View Horizon Environments, there is a vCenter Server available to be used with the Upgrade Manager. For manual upgrade methods, please refer to the VMware vSphere Upgrade Guide.

ESXi 6.0 hosts have the following requirements:

- For hardware support, ensure that all server and add-on cards are listed on the VMware Hardware Compatibility List: `http://www.vmware.com/resources/compatibility`.
- There must be two or more cores
- CPU must be 64-bit
- CPU must have been released after September 2006
- The CPU requires the NX/XD bit to be enabled on the CPU in the BIOs
- A minimum of 4 GB of RAM, ideally 24 GB or more for a VMware Horizon View Environment
- Must have Intel VT-x or AMD RVI available on the CPU (hardware virtualization)
- 1 or more Gigabit speed NICs, ideally two 10 Gb NICs

To upgrade the ESXi hosts to 6.0, ensure the environment meets the following criteria:

- All ESXi hosts must be 5.0 or later.
- Hosts must not have been upgraded from 3.0 or 4.0. If they were previously upgraded from these versions, a reinstall with the latest version will be required.
- All hosts must have a static IP or statically assigned DHCP address.
- **Disable Distributed Power Management (DPM).**
- Disable fault tolerance.
- Disable HA admission control.
- vCenter 6.0 and Upgrade Manager 6.0.

Upgrading the ESXi host will take approximately 15 to 30 minutes per host in the environment. Follow these steps to initiate a host upgrade:

1. Ensure that provisioning is disabled on the VMware Horizon View Environment, and that any pools with auto power on/always on have the feature disabled.

2. Upload the ESXi 6.0 image to the Update Manager; this can be done from the **ESXi Images** tab under the Update Manager Solution.

3. After the file is uploaded, click on **Next**.

4. Ensure **Create a baseline using the ESXi image** is selected and click on **Next**.

5. Specify the name and description for the upgrade baseline.

6. Switch to the **Hosts and Clusters** view.

7. Select the host or cluster you wish to upgrade and click on the **Update Manager** tab.

8. Click **Attach** in the upper-right corner.

9. In the **Attach Baseline or Group** window, select the baseline you created in step 4.

10. Click on **Attach**.

11. In the **Update Manager** tab, select **Scan...** to determine applicable updates/upgrades for the host.

12. Once the scan is complete, verify that an upgrade is available for the host. It should be indicated by a red x next to the baseline for the host.

13. Click on **Remediate...** to begin the host upgrade.

14. Accept the license agreement. Click on **Next**.

15. On the **Schedule** page, specify a name and description for the task, select **Immediately** to begin the process. Click on **Next**.

16. On the **Host Remediation Options** page, select the **Power state** dropdown menu. You can select the following options regarding the migration:

    ° **Power Off virtual machines**: Powers off the virtual machines and virtual appliances before remediation. If your virtual desktops are provisioned on local storage, this may be a good choice as those virtual desktops will not be able to be migrated without a View rebalance. Note that the vCenter/Update Manager must be on a host that is not being remediated for this to work.

    ° **Suspend virtual machines**: Suspends all running virtual machines and virtual appliances. Again, we need to ensure that the vCenter is migrated to another host prior to remediation.

    ◦ **Do not change VM power state**: Leaves the virtual machines in the current state. The host cannot enter maintenance mode until all the VMs are manually powered off, set to standby, or migrated to another host. Note that you will have to manually power off the virtual desktops on local storage.

17. Click on **Next**.

18. Enter the cluster remediation options:

    ◦ Disable **Distributed Power Management (DPM)**: Required for host upgrades.

    ◦ Disable **High Availability admission**: Required for host upgrades.

    ◦ Disable **Fault Tolerance (FT)**: Required for host upgrades.

    ◦ Enable parallel remediation for the hosts in the selected clusters: Optional; this setting will allow multiple hosts to be remediated simultaneously. This option should only be considered if you have greater than n+1 redundancy. Note that VSAN cannot be parallel remediated as it is only N+1 redundant by default. Update Manager will automatically limit parallel remediation to the maximum safe value.

    ◦ Migrate powered off and suspended virtual machines to other hosts in the cluster: Recommended for most environments, but may be disabled if the View desktops are provisioned with local storage.

19. Review the report. Click **Next**.

20. On the **Ready to Complete** page, click on **Finish**.

21. Wait for the hosts to enter maintenance mode. You may have to manually power off or migrate VMs pending on the previous options selected.

22. Once the host reboots you can power on or migrate VMs as needed.

23. Once all the hosts have been remediated to ESXi 6.0, we can move on to the next step.

For more details on the VMware ESXi upgrade process, please consult the following VMware guide:

`https://pubs.vmware.com/vsphere-60/topic/com.`
`vmware.ICbase/PDF/vsphere-esxi-vcenter-server-60-`
`upgrade-guide.pdf`

For a step by step guide you can visit:

`http://www.vladan.fr/patch-esxi-5-5-to-esxi-6-0/`

Upgrading VMware Tools and Horizon View agent on base image

Now that our hosts are upgraded to ESXi 6.0, we can go ahead and update our base images to the latest VMware tools. The VMware Tools upgrade is fairly straightforward. The VMware View agent has historically been dependent on the VMware tools, and as such it is recommended to uninstall the View agent prior to upgrading the VMware tools.

1. Download the VMware Horizon View agent from `https://my.vmware.com/`.

2. Power on the base image and log in.

3. Uninstall the VMware Horizon agent that exists on the base image.

4. Reboot the base image.

5. Log in and begin the VMware Tools upgrade. Automatic upgrade is acceptable, but a manual installation also works.

6. Reboot the base image.

7. Log in and begin the VMware Horizon agent installation. Make sure the executable and host bits match.

8. Follow the VMware Horizon View agent installation steps and click **Finish** when installed.

9. Shutdown the base image.

10. Take a snapshot of the base image.

11. Log into the VMware Horizon View administration view.

12. Navigate to the pool(s) in use.

13. Recompose the pool using the base image with the updated snapshot.

14. Monitor the recompose and verify the virtual desktop. Re-enter the available state.

Host upgrade planning

Whenever a host needs to be brought offline for maintenance or upgrades, there are a few basic things to be considered:

- Does the host have local storage virtual desktops? If yes, we need to power off the virtual desktops prior to putting the host in maintenance mode. Disabling "always power on" in the View Administrator console will prevent desktops from being powered on, on the host. Note that this requires a partial outage by getting the users affected by the outage to log off, and then log in to a virtual desktop on another host. Our other alternative is to schedule a maintenance window for the affected View pools.

- Is the host part of a Virtual SAN environment? If so, we will have to allocate time for the Virtual SAN to migrate data onto another host. The migration time will depend on the size of your Virtual SAN, and how fast the network interconnects are.

- For hardware support, ensure that all server and add-on cards are listed on the VMware hardware compatibility list: `http://www.vmware.com/resources/compatibility`.

Note the following should remain online for a host upgrade without a maintenance window:

- vCenter server must be operational throughout the host maintenance. Migrate the vCenter to other hosts as required.

- The View composer is usually installed on the vCenter and should be migrated with the vCenter.

- View connection server must be operational throughout the host maintenance. For redundant View connection servers, powering one down will result in approximately half the clients momentarily dropping a connection. Wherever possible, migrate the View connection server to another host.

- The View security server should also get the same treatment as the View connection server. Where possible migrate the View security server to another host prior to host maintenance.

- Note that redundant DNS and domain controllers can be powered off temporarily during a host outage.

Storage upgrade planning

Storage upgrades are trickier to plan without an outage window, as under most circumstances they require a rebalance operation. Whenever possible, use vStorage Motion to migrate the VMs to another datastore.

- Is the Horizon View installed on a Virtual SAN storage?

  Virtual SAN can be utilized to do storage maintenance without an outage. Virtual SAN can migrate all the data off a host without requiring a View rebalance operation.

- Is the storage deployed with redundant controllers?

  If the storage is deployed with redundant controllers and we are doing a controller maintenance, we can usually perform the maintenance action without taking down the host. Please consult with your storage vendor for more details regarding the maintenance action.

- Can we migrate the Horizon View environment to other storage?

  We can plan a View rebalance operation to migrate the virtual desktops to other storage. The rebalance will take 15–60 minutes, depending on the environment and the disk and CPU performance. During this time, virtual desktops affected by the rebalance will be unavailable.

- Are the view desktops fully provisioned?

  We can use vStorage Motion to migrate the desktops to another host without an outage.

Note that storage must always be available to the ESXi hosts with active VMs on it. Verify the datastore heartbeating options under **vSphere HA | Datastore Heartbeating** in the cluster properties window. You will want to ensure that any datastore undergoing maintenance is not configured to be a Heartbeating datastore.

Network upgrade planning

Network upgrades can be tricky with VMware Horizon View during the network upgrade; the following must remain in place for the environment to remain operational:

- Network connectivity between the vCenter and the ESXi hosts
- Network connectivity between the View composer and the View connection servers

- Network connectivity between the View connection servers and the virtual desktops
- Network connectivity between the View connection servers and the View security servers
- Network connectivity between all services and the DNS servers
- Network connectivity between all services and Active Directory domain controllers
- Network connectivity between the View connection servers and the clients
- Network connectivity between the View security servers and the clients
- Network connectivity between the ESXi hosts and any NFS or iSCSI storage

In practice, unless the upgrade can be accomplished without taking down the network, an outage will likely be required. During a network outage, the following should be set:

- For all linked-clone desktop pools, log into the View Administrator console and disable provisioning on the virtual machines.
- If any desktops are set to refresh the OS disk on logoff, set the **Refresh OS disk on logoff** setting to **Never**.
- Verify the behavior of the host isolation under **vSphere HA | Virtual Machine Options** in the cluster settings. Most likely, you will want the host isolation configured to keep the VMs on during an outage for the duration of the network maintenance.

This will prevent boot storm issues when the network comes back and will reduce potential problems that may occur.

Summary

In this chapter, we covered the upgrade and installation of VMware Horizon View, VMware vCenter, and basic host and storage upgrade planning. We covered the basic upgrade requirements and planned ahead with ideas to speed up the View upgrades. We covered networking, storage, and host upgrade planning and covered common pitfalls to prevent issues during the upgrade.

Index

Thank you for buying
VMware Horizon View High Availability

About Packt Publishing

Packt, pronounced 'packed', published its first book, *Mastering phpMyAdmin for Effective MySQL Management*, in April 2004, and subsequently continued to specialize in publishing highly focused books on specific technologies and solutions.

Our books and publications share the experiences of your fellow IT professionals in adapting and customizing today's systems, applications, and frameworks. Our solution-based books give you the knowledge and power to customize the software and technologies you're using to get the job done. Packt books are more specific and less general than the IT books you have seen in the past. Our unique business model allows us to bring you more focused information, giving you more of what you need to know, and less of what you don't.

Packt is a modern yet unique publishing company that focuses on producing quality, cutting-edge books for communities of developers, administrators, and newbies alike. For more information, please visit our website at www.packtpub.com.

About Packt Enterprise

In 2010, Packt launched two new brands, Packt Enterprise and Packt Open Source, in order to continue its focus on specialization. This book is part of the Packt Enterprise brand, home to books published on enterprise software – software created by major vendors, including (but not limited to) IBM, Microsoft, and Oracle, often for use in other corporations. Its titles will offer information relevant to a range of users of this software, including administrators, developers, architects, and end users.

Writing for Packt

We welcome all inquiries from people who are interested in authoring. Book proposals should be sent to author@packtpub.com. If your book idea is still at an early stage and you would like to discuss it first before writing a formal book proposal, then please contact us; one of our commissioning editors will get in touch with you.

We're not just looking for published authors; if you have strong technical skills but no writing experience, our experienced editors can help you develop a writing career, or simply get some additional reward for your expertise.

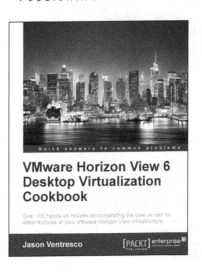

VMware Horizon View 6 Desktop Virtualization Cookbook

ISBN: 978-1-78217-164-5   Paperback: 332 pages

Over 100 hands-on recipes demonstrating the core as well as latest features of your VMware Horizon View infrastructure

1. Gain a detailed insight into the configuration and administration of core features of VMware Horizon View.

2. Learn how to deploy the newest features of the VMware Horizon View 6.0 such as Cloud Pod Architecture, VSAN integration, and more.

3. Benefit from practical examples that provide a greater level of detail than the VMware Horizon View documentation.

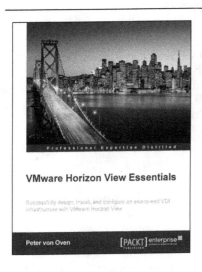

VMware Horizon View Essentials

ISBN: 978-1-78439-936-8   Paperback: 252 pages

Successfully design, install, and configure an end-to-end VDI infrastructure with VMware Horizon View

1. Learn how to design, implement, secure, and optimize the performance of a VDI project.

2. Revolutionize the way you manage your desktop infrastructure, while delivering a superior user experience.

3. Step-by-step guide and provides screen shots that allow you to follow and set up your lab, complete with real-life scenarios.

Please check **www.PacktPub.com** for information on our titles

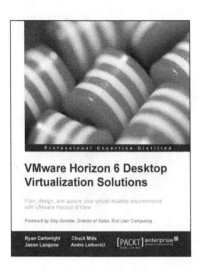

VMware Horizon View 6 Desktop Virtualization Solutions

ISBN: 978-1-78217-070-9   Paperback: 362 pages

Plan, design, and secure your virtual desktop environments with VMware Horizon 6 View

1. Design a successful solution to deliver Windows desktops and applications as a service.

2. Provide redundancy for components and design a backup solution and disaster recovery plan to protect your investment and to keep your users productive.

3. A learn-by-example-based approach that focuses on key concepts to provide the foundation to solve real-world problems.

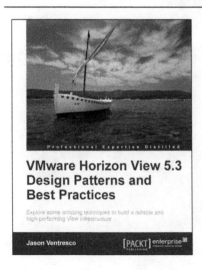

VMware Horizon View 5.3 Design Patterns and Best Practices

ISBN: 978-1-78217-154-6   Paperback: 124 pages

Explore some amazing techniques to build a reliable and high-performing View infrastructure

1. Identify the reasons why you are deploying Horizon View, a critical step to identifying your metrics for success.

2. Determine your Horizon View desktop resource requirements, and use that to size your infrastructure.

3. Recognize key design considerations that should influence your Horizon View infrastructure.

Please check **www.PacktPub.com** for information on our titles